Can the Internet Strengthen Democracy?

T0044960

Stephen Coleman

———————

Can the Internet Strengthen Democracy?

polity

First published in 2017 by Polity Press

Polity Press
65 Bridge Street
Cambridge CB2 1UR, UK

Polity Press
350 Main Street
Malden, MA 02148, USA

ISBN-13: 978-1-5095-0836-5
ISBN-13: 978-1-5095-0837-2 (pb)

A catalogue record for this book is available from the British Library.

Typeset in 11 on 15 pt Sabon
by Toppan Best-set Premedia Limited
Printed and bound in Great Britain by CPI Group (UK) Ltd, Croydon.

The publisher has used its best endeavours to ensure that the URLs for external websites referred to in this book are correct and active at the time of going to press. However, the publisher has no responsibility for the websites and can make no guarantee that a site will remain live or that the content is or will remain appropriate.

Every effort has been made to trace all copyright holders, but if any have been inadvertently overlooked the publisher will be pleased to include any necessary credits in any subsequent reprint or edition.

For further information on Polity, visit our website: politybooks.com

Contents

Preface

I began writing this book in the months leading up to the jolt of Brexit and concluded the final passages shortly after the thud of the Trump victory. During these turbulent months I observed how information was routinely distorted, public debate was impoverished and voting citizens were infantilized. I was left with the strong feeling that democracy deserved better than this; and, in particular, that spaces for meaningful and consequential public exchange of ideas and experiences were in worryingly short supply.

As populism has prospered, filling the void created by the sterility of 'politics as usual', some critics have blamed the Internet for giving undeserved prominence to the raucous claims of know-nothing bigots and cynical fake news purveyors. Others argue that the digital circulation of non-elite voices constitutes the best opportunity available of denting the dominance of mass-media-framed reality. My aim in writing this book has been to move the debate away from what the Internet *does to* democracy and open a discussion about the kind of democracy we want to *make for ourselves*.

Of three things we can be sure. Firstly, the Internet does not shape democracy, but, like every medium before it, from the alphabet to television, is shaped by the ways that society chooses to use its available tools. Secondly, the Internet will not go away. Even if one were to accept the alarmist claims that digital technologies are producing new generations of distracted, inconsiderate, gullible addicts, the solution is unlikely to lie in undoing the popularity of the Internet. Thirdly, just as the Internet is not a fixed entity with pre-determined effects, neither is democracy. Indeed, the main argument of the pages that follow is that reconfiguring democratic politics is even more important than coming to terms with the Internet as a feature of our age.

*

I am grateful to Louise Knight and her colleagues at Polity Press for encouraging me to reflect upon the political and moral significance of the Internet.

Preface

I have spent much of the past two decades attempting to make sense of what the Internet might mean for the distribution and exercise of political power. Over those years, I have benefited from the intellectual stimulus of friends and associates, including my former colleagues at the Oxford Internet Institute and the many staff and students with whom I now have the pleasure of interacting in the School of Media and Communication at the University of Leeds.

Jay Blumler and John Corner will find their intellectual imprints in this text, but are certainly not responsible for its shortcomings. I am grateful to Victoria Jaynes for being a terrific research assistant, to Justin Dyer for copy-editing the text so very diligently and to Simon Osler for being an excellent guide to online political sources. As ever, Bernadette Coleman has been invaluable in helping to shape my thinking.

The period in which this book was written has been a worrying one for those of us who believe that democracy amounts to more than the tyranny of deluded majorities. This book is dedicated to those who share these worries and are prepared to take a stand for something better.

1

The Great Missed Opportunity

Governments across the world, in both established and new democracies, have missed a huge opportunity to reinvent themselves, restore their legitimacy and connect with citizens. In the mid-1990s, as governments faced a global wave of disaffection and disengagement, a new public communication network emerged: the Internet. Since then, a range of social relationships – from friendship ties to market transactions to knowledge acquisition – have been transformed. Democratic governance is an exception to those transformations. There has been no shortage of e-rhetoric from governments at all levels (local, national and transnational), but in practice an ethos of centralized institutionalism has prevailed.

Democratic governments find themselves confused and embarrassed by the ubiquity of the

Internet. There is a fundamental mismatch between its logic and theirs. Meanwhile, forms of communication with government that dominated the pre-Internet era – parties, the broadcast media and newspapers – are in decline, particularly in relation to the generation that has grown to adulthood in the past twenty years.

While institutions stagger from strategy to strategy, not capable of living with the Internet and not able to live without it, citizens are engaging with one another online in imaginative and efficacious ways. Horizontal (peer-to-peer) citizenship seems to be alive and well, while vertical (top-down) citizenship seems to be clogged up and unappealing.

Defined for the purpose of this book as a network of interconnected computer networks comprising a range of platforms, devices and protocols facilitating a global flow of data that can be used, shared, stored and retrieved by users, the Internet has come to symbolize contemporary aspirations to communicate without restraint. Attempts to evaluate the social significance of the Internet have prompted a framing war between those who regard late modernity as an era of listless decadence characterized by endless opportunities for people to speak without listening and those who discern progressive potential in the relentless advance of global integration and its attendant networks of interdependent but uncoordinated communication. Much of the scholarly literature has been dominated by those who believe that the Internet will fundamentally transform political democracy, replacing old forms of representation with new systems of plebiscitary technopopulism, and those who believe that digital politics will merely replicate long-established structural forms and conventions, shooing innovation to the margins. Fragments of hard evidence can be found to support both of these accounts (certainly enough to fill several half-persuasive books), but such arguments are ultimately strained and almost obsessive in their eagerness to excite or deny.

Both sides in this somewhat sterile debate argue about the Internet's role in recent historical events, from the election of the first black American President to the insurgent vibrancy of the Arab Spring. Rather like a group of historians arguing about whether access to the printing press did or did not cause the revolutions that swept across Europe in 1848, the impossibility of arriving at an intelligent answer lies in the vapidity of the question. Historical change is rarely dependent upon just one factor. Historical agency does not reside in artefacts. Claims that the Internet changes everything or that it changes nothing in the political (or any other) sphere are of little value, for they over-state the powers of technology, reducing history to a crude study of media effects.

Rather more interesting analyses are likely to emerge when, instead of asking whether the Internet does this or that to politics, we ask what kind of challenges political democracy currently faces and how, shaped by conscious human intervention, the Internet – or at least some of its features – might be utilized in tackling them. Consider two critical challenges facing both long-established and newly formed democracies throughout the contemporary world. Firstly, the problem of making democratic representation meaningful to people. How, instead of regarding representative institutions, such as congresses and parliaments, as remote, unintelligible, self-serving and insensitive to mundane experience, could represented citizens come to feel that they are – or, at least, could be – an integral part of the democratic process? Arguably, unless such a relationship can be fostered, the legitimacy of democratic governance will continue to atrophy and the capacity of elected leaders to depend upon the consent of citizens will be undermined. Secondly, a fundamental challenge facing anyone wanting to engage in collective political action is the problem of coordination. Put simply, it is much easier for people with many resources (money, status, networks) to work together towards a political end than those with access to few. A billionaire hedge-fund investor has few difficulties finding or meeting with others sharing the same material interest. They can jump on a plane, hire a hotel for an international conference, pay lobbyists to put pressure on governments and publicize their cause. An office cleaner on a zero-hours contract will find it more difficult to connect and organize with others in the same position. It is not easy to reach cleaners in other office blocks (less still in other countries), to find places to meet, money to sustain and publicize a campaign or confidence to deal with the risk of personal recrimination. Traditionally, the capacity of richer, higher-status, more confident people to mobilize resources for collective action has resulted in an unequal political playing field. Although many disadvantaged groups do engage in collective action, often with considerable success, the practical barriers to coordination make it harder for them to combine their efforts than it is for the more affluent.

Faced with these barriers, some thinkers and practitioners have turned to the Internet, not as a technocratic panacea for the shortcomings of democracy, but as a contribution to the reconfiguration of political practice. Rather than claiming that the Internet 'makes things happen', they have sought ways of exploiting it in the service of democratic agency. Let's consider in some detail two of the most thoughtful and comprehensive recent attempts to demonstrate a positive link between the Internet and reinvigorated democracy. The first relates to the challenge of making representative institutions more open to public understanding, scrutiny and input. The second relates to the potential of digital technologies to overcome hitherto intractable barriers to political coordination and collective action.

Putting Parliament online?

Who better to initiate a programme designed to make parliamentary democracy more transparent, accessible and interactive than the Speaker of the British House of Commons? This is an old legislature which has withstood the arrival and consolidation of previous communication revolutions, such as the printing press and broadcasting. Suffused by tradition and somewhat resistant to the flurried rhetoric of modernization, the UK Parliament has been slow to adjust to the expectations of digitally experienced citizens. It has had its own website since 1996 and engaged in some experiments in e-consultation, but its sense of what it means to represent millions of people seems not to have changed much since before the advent of television. When the Speaker of the House of Commons, John Bercow, established a Digital Democracy Commission 'to consider, report and make recommendations on how parliamentary democracy in the United Kingdom can embrace the opportunities afforded by the digital world to become more effective in making laws, scrutinising the work and performance of government, representing citizens, encouraging citizens to engage with democracy and facilitating dialogue amongst citizens', this was regarded by political insiders as a potentially significant initiative. It was not to be a merely speculative exercise, but a project intended to achieve outcomes that would refresh the terms of democratic representation. The Commission took a year to collect evidence and produce recommendations, which were published in January 2015 in a report entitled *Open Up!*[1]

The Commission's acknowledgement that the Internet was not a cure-all for the problems of representative democracy was reassuring: 'One message that resonated very clearly was that digital is only part of the answer. It can help to make democratic processes easier for people to understand and take part in, but other barriers must also be addressed for digital to have a truly transformative effect.'[2] Equally impressive was the Commission's commitment to 'the need for Parliament to develop an appetite for risk-taking and innovation, which is an essential component of doing digital well'.[3] And, indeed, the Commission did come up with a range of worthy and sometimes ambitious recommendations to be acted upon between now and the next general election. If implemented effectively, the Commission's proposals would be likely to make the UK Parliament much better at telling its own story, appearing more open to public scrutiny and avoiding the risk of seeming to be behind the curve of other institutions with which people interact in their daily lives.

Missing from the Commission's report, however, is any consideration of what democratic representation means and how the terms of such a relationship might be changing. Institutional roles and practices in contexts ranging from healthcare to education to journalism have been reconceived in recent years, problematizing relations between experts and lay audiences, formal and vernacular expression, epistemological authority and plurality, and dissemination and gatekeeping. Why should political representation be any different?

The Great Missed Opportunity

Historically, political representatives have been products of distance, appointed or elected to travel to capital cities, there to speak for the people who could not make the journey to faraway royal courts and legislatures. As politics became more institutionalized and the franchise broadened, political representatives came to be regarded as bridges of cognitive as well as geographical distance. Lacking the time or knowledge to engage fully in the technicalities of policy formation and decision-making, people relied on political representatives to think through complex questions on their behalf. In time, the role became professionalized and politicians began to be accused of embodying the very distance they were supposed to be reconciling. The inherent tension between representation as substitution and simulacrum moved too far towards the former. Nowadays, political representatives are commonly accused of not listening to the people they represent; having partisan loyalties that casually override local mandates; taking citizens for granted; and emerging from such a narrow social base that they neither resemble nor empathize with the people they are supposed to be speaking for. At the same time, representative institutions seem to have lost their way: sometimes a perfunctory mechanism for the rubber-stamping of executive decisions; at other times an irrelevant theatre of circumscribed authority.

Can such relationships of distance be sustained in the era of the Internet? When the physical journey between institutional centres and the communities in which people live and work are transcended by technologies that compress time and shrink space, is it still meaningful to think of representatives as having to rely on four- or five-yearly elections to know what the represented think? When political information is so abundantly available and openly contested, do we still need specialist experts in deliberation to make judgements on behalf of citizens? When it is often easier for community members to discuss issues with one another than with their elected representative, can the latter's preferences and values be regarded as inherently worthier of legislative enactment than those of organized communities?

Some have responded to these questions by concluding that the age of political representation is passing.[4] There is, however, no evidence of any public appetite for ongoing direct democracy – and most of the early arguments for push-button e-democracy have been strikingly insensitive to the intense intricacies that characterize complex political disagreement. Rather than displacing political

10

representation, digital communication technologies point towards innovative ways of spanning the distance between everyday experience and democratic governance.

Openness to such change is less a matter of embracing apps and software codes than of acknowledging the two-sidedness of the democratic relationship. Contemporary political representation is characterized by an acute imbalance of voice. Democratic governance, which is supposed to place citizens at the centre of the social stage, routinely casts them as muted extras. Public talk is too often suffocated by elite speechifying. The political sphere is dominated by overbearing voices, all too often consumed by agendas that seem narrowly tactical and self-referential.

And yet a conspicuous characteristic of late-modern culture is the presence of voluble, non-deferential publics. There are very few matters that people will not talk about these days, and there are lots of places to do so, especially online. Compared with previous generations, in which teenagers couldn't talk openly about sex, deferential workers were trained to know their place and doff their caps to their masters, the frightened middle class vowed never to talk religion or politics in public, and debate on radio and television resembled Oxbridge senior common rooms, the vivacity and sheer volume of twenty-first-century talk is striking. Elitist critics complain that such political talk can be strident and ill informed, but this is to miss what is really important: a growing sense that to be a democratic citizen entails a commitment to be heard rather than retreat into the passive whispers of the default follower. In the main, politicians and political institutions have not adapted well to this new environment, remaining conspicuously monological in their expressive performances and failing to exhibit the characteristics of good listeners. While more astute politicians speak of their commitment to 'conversation' with the people they represent, they have been slow to engage with the techniques and technologies of multi-vocal interaction that make social media so appealing.

This points towards the case for a dialogical form of political representation, based more on the potential for communicative interaction than the intractability of distance. Indeed, the report of the Speaker's Digital Democracy Commission gestures towards such a development, stating that a

> big advantage of social media is that people can respond to meetings and events in their own words. Up-to-the-minute information about Parliament

does not need to be one-way. Currently, members of the public who watch parliamentary debates are not allowed to use their phones. But people increasingly expect to be able to tweet and blog live from these kinds of events. Allowing people to take mobile devices in with them would allow them to do this.[5]

But this important acknowledgement of the value of people's 'own words' envisages a purely responsive role for them: commenting on meetings and events in which politicians are speaking; tweeting and blogging as they *watch* Parliament at work. What about the voices of citizens as contributors to scrutiny, policy thinking and deliberation? On this, the report takes a much more guarded tone: 'We are confident that online participation by the public in the work of Parliament will be increasingly important, but we have deliberately set out a cautious approach to this, at least initially, to avoid early experiments being crushed by the weight of expectations.'[6] So cautious, indeed, that the only references in the report to public input to political representation refer to e-petitions, in which people are allowed to sign a proposal without any further interaction with other signatories or parliamentarians, and the rather tokenistic suggestion that members of the public could be allowed to discuss issues online before they are debated in the House of Commons overflow chamber, Westminster Hall: 'People interested in the topic for debate should have the opportunity to discuss it online, before the House of Commons debate. MPs could contribute or simply observe.'[7] People interested in parliamentary debates are already free to discuss them online before they take place and MPs are already free to participate in such discussions, which few do, preferring to observe them from a distance at best or ignore them as irrelevant interventions.

The report cites 'expert evidence' stating that 'technology is "excellent at gathering information", [but] it is still not very good at large-scale deliberation'.[8] What exactly does this mean? Technology is not an agent: it neither gathers information nor determines the quality of public deliberation. Perhaps the more candid claim being made here is that citizens are quite capable of gathering information about what politicians are saying and doing, but not very good at deliberating with one another about important political issues. Whatever the intended meaning, it would have been useful to hear from the Commission about whether and how democratic representation could be strengthened by a more ongoing exchange of ideas, knowledge and experience between representatives and the people they speak for.

Failing to think through – or even fleetingly address – opportunities for the potential of a radically updated democratic relationship, the Commission focused its energies on finding ways to make citizens understand the current parliamentary process, as if lifting the parliamentary veil and allowing citizens to follow the proceedings of their rulers would be sufficient to overcome feelings of estrangement: 'The Commission was struck by the effect that...lack of understanding has on our democratic system, with many citizens feeling disconnected from MPs and Parliament. We welcome the ongoing work to increase public understanding of Parliament....'[9] 'Perhaps the biggest barrier to engaging with Parliament and politics that young people experience is a lack of knowledge about political and parliamentary processes. That is why we are recommending that political education should be improved.'[10]

One of the report's more innovative proposals was to establish a 'jargon-busting' tool that will help citizens to make sense of what their representatives are saying and doing: 'Making parliamentary language more accessible will be central to opening up Parliament. Digital tools such as jargon busters could help people to understand complex parliamentary language.'[11] The idea that political miscommunication can be overcome by providing citizens with digital phrasebooks, as if they were stumbling tourists on an exotic voyage, rather misses the point. Perhaps it is representatives who should be issued with digital 'jargon-busters' to assist them in communicating reciprocally with the many social groups whose interests and views are under-represented in the corridors of power. Meaningful translation is a two-way street, and self-referential appeals to 'understand us as we wish to be understood' fail to address what would seem to be the more intractable aspect of the crisis of representation. The Commission has set Parliament the ambitious 'challenge of ensuring that by 2020 everyone can understand what it does',[12] but might it be that a more urgent democratic challenge would be for parliamentarians to find better ways of understanding what citizens ('everyone') do, say and want – to close the glaring gap between politics (institutional, top-down) and democracy (grass-roots, ground-up)?

Coordinating political protest

Engaging with conventional political institutions is not the only way for citizens to make their voices heard. As faith in formal politics has waned, the appeal of democratic activities that work around and beyond traditional political institutions has grown. Networked forms of social communication have enabled twenty-first-century activists to combine online coordination and street-level action to set agendas, register influence and enact protest. More extensive, instantaneous and innovatory than most institutional uses of the Internet, digital activism relies upon a form of political energy that leaves old-fashioned politics seeming sluggish and stale. Rather than waiting for representatives to speak for them, digital activists have fine-tuned dynamic practices of self-representation.

In doing so, they have had to address the historic challenge of coordination. Both scholars and practitioners have sensed that there is something about the Internet that makes it possible for groups with few resources, flexible structures and evolving programmes to coordinate for collective action, but it is only recently that this phenomenon has been systematically theorized. W. Lance Bennett and Alexandra Segerberg's book *The Logic of Connective Action: Digital Media and the Personalization of Contentious Politics*, which is based on extensive empirical evidence from new social movements such as the Spanish *indignados* and Occupy, has been rightly regarded as a groundbreaking attempt to reconceive collective action for the digital age. Bennett and Segerberg show in great detail how digital technologies enable people with similar problems or goals to join together without being managed by centralized party or movement leaderships. It is impossible to do complete justice here to this carefully constructed theory, but the nub of Bennett and Segerberg's argument is that

> When interpersonal networks are enabled by technology platforms of various designs that coordinate and scale the networks, the resulting action can resemble collective action, yet without the same role played by formal organizations or the need for exclusive, collective action framings. In place of content that is distributed and relationships that are brokered by hierarchical organizations, connective action networks involve co-production and co-distribution, revealing different economic and psychological logic: peer production based on sharing and personalized expression.[13]

As a consequence, democratic action becomes easier to coordinate, less oppressively binding to engage in and capable of morphing flexibly between related issues. Bennett and Segerberg cite compelling examples of connective action, ranging from social movements that emerged in response to the financial crash to the adoption of novel and flexible organizational strategies by third-sector organizations. As connective action gathers traction with many citizens, especially younger people who are attracted to the versatility of 'DIY politics',[14] older forms of collective action are looking increasingly creaky and incapable of realizing democratic expectations. Why sit in a draughty room once a week to go through the tedious agenda of a local party branch when one can connect with like-minded people online and choose to engage with them in face-to-face actions when needed? The performative appeal of connective action is almost the exact opposite of the civic spectatorship afforded to people seeking to interact with parliaments and governments. Connective action's focus upon 'organizing without organizations'[15] points towards a new way of thinking about what it means to be politically engaged.

Even the most pessimistic critic of the Internet as a political resource would find it hard to deny that, while problems of democratic coordination have not been eradicated, digital networks have expanded the range of voices available to be heard within the public sphere; made it easier for solidarities to emerge, often of global proportions; and made it much harder for entrenched interests to ignore dissenting actors as if they did not exist. The rich and powerful use the Internet, as they have always used resources, to consolidate and intensify their socio-political advantages, but they are increasingly troubled by the scope for contention and disclosure generated by the weakening of media gatekeeping. It is more difficult than ever to claim to represent people while ignoring their interests and preferences, and it is easier than ever before for the misrepresented to coordinate with a view to making their own claims.

All of that is normatively good for democracy. But there are limits to connective action. The capacity to initiate and sustain forms of political action based on the coordination of dispersed energy is a vital precondition for democratic efficacy, but only a precondition. There is a significant difference between short-term mobilization and long-term policy formation. Setting a radical counter-agenda is one thing; turning it into a framework for policy implementation is another. Without effective mobilization, durable political impacts are unlikely to be realized; but with only vibrant mobilization, democratic energy can all too easily be dissipated.

At stake here is a fundamental tension at the heart of democratic politics between inputs and outputs. Inputs refer to the expression of political demands.

The Great Missed Opportunity

The democratic quality of inputs can be evaluated in terms of the extent to which they are arrived at and supported fairly, reflectively and inclusively. Outputs refer to the decisions and actions of political authorities: the policies that are implemented and the social effects that are realized. The democratic quality of outputs is best evaluated in terms of the extent to which they reflect public inputs. A political system that encourages public input into the policy process but ignores such input when it comes to producing outputs lacks democratic legitimacy. Likewise, a political system that limits policy inputs to elites can never be fully democratic, even if its policy outputs are bureaucratically effective in keeping the public content. This tension is acknowledged by the leading theorist of network politics, Manuel Castells, who notes that 'the critical passage from hope to implantation of change depends on the permeability of political institutions to the demands of the movement and on the willingness of the movement to engage in a process of negotiation'.[16] Such negotiations are often doomed to failure from the outset because online networked movements do not trust state-centred political arrangements:

> Movements do not object to the principle of representative democracy, but denounce the practice of

> such democracy as it is today, and do not recognize
> its legitimacy. Under such conditions, there is little
> chance of a positive direct interaction between
> movements and the political class.... Since the road
> to policy changes goes through political change, and
> political change is shaped through the interests of
> the politicians in charge, the influence of the move-
> ment on policy is usually limited, at least in the
> short term, in the absence of a major crisis that
> requires the overhaul of the entire system....[17]

This amounts to rather more than a glib critique of
the failure of social movements to bring about
wholesale global transformation. The problem is
not that connective action is impotent (few would
deny the significance of the global spread of Occupy's 'We are the 99%' meme or the effective ways
in which WikiLeaks disrupted hegemonic narratives), but that the process of bringing about policy
changes at state and transnational levels entails
long-term, strategic engagement with political elites
that are characteristically hierarchical, impersonal
and insensible to lay knowledgeabilities. Even
when they are supported by substantial networks,
advocates of social change are unlikely to penetrate
elite structures through the force of moral narrative. Connective action may be good at mobilizing
radical inputs, but it offers no mechanism for

translating them into outputs. Waiting for 'a major crisis that requires the overhaul of the entire system'[18] is one option for connective activists, but a more constructive alternative to such apocalypticism would be to seek ways to democratize the decision-making process itself so that public will can be transfigured into sustainable policies. But this would entail a commitment to a much less ephemeral conception of political radicalism than that which characterizes contemporary connective action.

A dialectical approach

In reviewing these recent attempts to demonstrate a positive link between the Internet and reinvigorated democracy, firstly by modernizing institutional representation and secondly by acknowledging enhanced opportunities for coordination and collective action, we seem to have encountered two visions of democracy, each struggling in their own way for legitimacy and efficacy, each latching on to digital technology as a means of limping forward without having to collaborate with the other. Parliamentary representatives want citizens to know and understand them. Connective actors want the political elite to feel their presence. Proponents of each vision invoke their own framing metaphors. Top-down democrats summon up the image of the political citadel unlocked, with citizens invited to take their place in a digitally equipped spectators' gallery. Ground-up democrats conjure up images of permanent, ever-expanding mobilization, horizontally connected, but vertically somewhat adrift.

How can these divergent potentialities be reconciled? That is the question that must be answered if the relationship between the Internet and democracy is not to be dissipated in a succession of abortive attempts to redress discrete inadequacies of practice. Those who see digital communication technologies as means of bolstering failing institutions and unjustifiable hierarchies are unlikely to have anything useful to say about how the Internet might strengthen democracy. They are too locked into obsolete rituals of industrial-model governance. Those who see the Internet as somehow prefiguring a post-political universe in which 'all may enter without privilege or prejudice accorded by race, economic power, military force, or station of birth'[19] will inevitably be disappointed. Communication technologies do not make or displace political reality, but can only ever play a part in the efforts of conscious agents to create a richer

24

democracy than the one we have now. The democratic theorist John Keane has observed that

> [w]hen faced with unfamiliar situations, it is always tempting to suppose that new media will carry on doing familiar things…, but in more efficient and effective, faster and cheaper ways….The enticement should be resisted. Presumptions that have outlived their usefulness must be abandoned. What is needed are bold new probes, fresh-minded perspectives, 'wild' concepts that enable different and meaningful ways of seeing things, more discriminating methods of recognising the novelties of our times, the democratic opportunities they offer and the counter-trends that have the potential to snuff out democratic politics.[20]

Following this wise advice entails a fine balance between acknowledging the institutional entrenchment and resilience of actually existing democracy and apprehending the scope for new democratic values, practices and connections that accord with the novelties of our times. This means asking fundamental questions about the sort of world we want to live in; the kind of politics that would serve us well; and the ways in which information and communication technologies might help us to realize our humanity. It means asking whether we really want to strengthen democracy or whether we are prepared to define ourselves by democratic principles that are mainly observed in the breach. It means asking: Even if the Internet could help to make the political sphere more inclusive, are we sure that we want it to be inclusive? Do we really value all voices and want to learn from the widest range of human experiences? These are questions that should not be overlooked, thereby ignoring the many powerful voices lined up against democracy, in substance if not in name. Given that anxieties about the inanity and irresponsibility of the online public feature so commonly in discussions about the Internet, it would be useful to see whether such unease is unique to our own times or whether its roots are rather deeper. And given that the Internet is the most recent in a long line of communication technologies that have been seen as having far-reaching political effects, it makes sense to ask how the previous technology, television, was evaluated as a democratic medium when it first came on to the scene. The next chapter turns to a consideration of those questions. In the chapter after that, attention turns to the various ways in which conventional political communication practices in established democracies have changed in the era of the Internet. It is a story of incremental modifications rather than comprehensive transformation. There is now an extensive research literature that explores the range and depth of these changes, but the combined narrative has something of a piecemeal quality – an account of grudging institutional accommodation to an emergent media ecology; of pilot exercises and experiments that rarely persist beyond the point of tentative findings; of big ideas enervated by bureaucratic implementation; and of technocratic solutions in collision with political logic. It would be a pity to conclude the analysis at that point. And that is why the final chapter engages with the call for wild and imaginative thinking, untrammelled by the strictures of political convention, while acknowledging that certain features of democracy – representation, elections, nation states – are likely to persist into the future, even if in an altered form. Adopting such an approach entails thinking rather less about how the Internet affects democracy and more about how democracy and technology are dialectically entwined. Democracy is not enacted and then mediated. It is performed through acts of mediation. Technologies of mediation are and always have been inherent in the social enactment of democracy. Whether the Internet can help to strengthen democracy depends, therefore, upon the kind of democracy we want to strengthen.

2

Political Hopes and Fears

What's gone wrong with democracy?

Democracy arises from an instinct that the exercise of power should be accountable to those who are affected by it; that arbitrary authority is inherently suspect and the expression of public voice never an unwelcome transgression. The foundational principle of democracy is that the interests and values of society should be collectively, self-consciously and autonomously determined by citizens rather than ordained by elites.

The historical link between how societies communicate and how they govern themselves has always been critical. Technologies and practices of communication are more than a means of delivering political messages. They are a key determinant in shaping the ways in which power is exercised. For

28

democracy to be more than an empty label, there must exist modes of communication that enable the people (or *demos*) to exercise unconstrained agency. Because democratic judgement is always generated intersubjectively, rather than through the whim of autocrats, it must be supported by communicative structures, styles and habits that are oriented towards democratic norms.

At this moment in the early twenty-first century, while democracy continues to have great purchase as a rhetorical trope, there is a growing unease that substantive social power resides beyond the control of the *demos*, wielded by unaccountable global forces and elusive domestic elites. The conduct of politics appears to be a Machiavellian contest for power: a game of thrones; a contest for commanding influence. Winning political battles seems to be mainly a matter of calculated endeavour and subtle cunning on the part of elites and their often cynical strategists. To act 'politically' has come to mean operating with an eye to manipulative advantage; to sacrifice veracity for plausibility.

While the promise of democratic politics is that all members of society, regardless of their socio-economic status, are free to address and remedy problems that affect them, there is a widespread perception that policies are constructed and decisions made over the heads of the public. People acknowledge that they have the right to vote for their chosen representatives and preferred policies (and that this is certainly more democratic than the denial of such an opportunity), and yet they feel that the really important decisions that affect their lives are not only made without their involvement, but are often made in ways that leave them feeling like beguiled and confused onlookers. Much policy formation and decision-making is complex and opaque, taking place within unaccountable institutions, such as the International Monetary Fund, the World Bank, the European Commission, multinational corporations and the amorphous and all-powerful 'markets'. Policy agendas are either hard to fathom (especially through the claims and counter-claims of rival politicians) or too narrowly conceived, failing to include some of the more intuitively sensible options that are ruled out as being 'unrealistic'. Choices between policy X and policy Z turn into contests for the least awful option. Political democracy begins to feel like shopping in a very bad supermarket where the daily choice is between what's not available and what you don't really want.

At the same time, democratic politics is marred by a conspicuous deficit of trust. When people are presented with 'facts', 'narratives' and 'advice' by governments, political leaders and other centres of authority, they do not know what to believe. Most of us would prefer to assume that what others tell us is well intentioned and valid, but experience teaches us to doubt some sources more than others. Disbelieving what political leaders say has now become almost a default setting. 'Speaking like a politician' has become a popular euphemism for distorting the truth or plain lying. Confronted with the challenge of working out whether we are being told the truth by political leaders, citizens must become expert decoders. For politicians are particularly good at seeming to say things that turn out, upon scrutiny, to mean something quite different. In some cases their speech is manipulative or evasive. Often they will say (or appear to say) one thing to one audience and something rhetorically different to another. 'We have no current plans to...' might mean that 'We almost certainly will have plans to next year.' 'This policy is based on the best expert advice we could find' might be translated as 'We managed to find one expert out of many who thinks that this policy could just possibly work.' Sometimes a politician will explain a policy clearly and compellingly, only to be followed by another politician – or political commentator – who points out the half-truths, evidential gaps and internal contradictions of what had a few moments earlier seemed convincing. All of this becomes rather wearying for people after a while. Life seems to be too short to decode the endless political-speak of professional politicians. If only the whole process could be slowed down.

For it takes time, effort and focus to work out what to think about the vast array of issues that dominate the political sphere. It is easy to be confused or discouraged by the sheer complexity of the political agenda, and yet opportunities to arrive at a considered judgement through discussion with others are few and far between. The aim of market-oriented political communication is to sell the brand (be it a candidate, party or policy) rather than to invite people to compare the pros and cons of competing positions. As political talk becomes more strident and uncivil, there is a diminishing scope for finding common ground, making sense of radically opposing values and being open to perspectives emanating from quite different life experiences. What commonly passes for political debate takes place in TV and radio studios where a narrow cast of skilled tacticians seem to limbo-dance under the questions posed to them while doing their best to ignore, put down or interrupt their opponents. People who do not follow this sort of bizarre point-scoring as a hobby are inclined to switch off and tune out. Most people sense that a political system in which everyone has the right to vote, but nobody has time or space to reflect on their own opinions or listen to others, is a rather hollow version of democracy. The missing element of contemporary political democracy is deliberation: the opportunity to share, compare, argue and resolve views with others. For deliberation to be effective, it must be socially cross-cutting, bringing together diverse individuals, communities and perspectives into a respectful public dialogue. Where is there to go in contemporary society to engage in this kind of meaningful deliberation? Try typing into Google a request for the location of your nearest deliberative forum. You will easily find your nearest betting shop, lap-dancing club or cash converter, but the absence of any recognized spaces for public delib-eration tells its own story.

Added to all of this is a prevalent sense that the loudest and most powerful voices in political parties, campaigns and media debates reflect certain social groups more than others. Those who are richer, more educationally qualified and more culturally confident are significantly more likely to join politi-cal parties, vote in elections, participate in govern-ment consultations and enjoy success in lobbying for their own interests and opposing decisions not in line with their interests or values. In Britain, there is just a 34 per cent probability that an individual under the age of 35, earning less than £10,000 a year, will vote, whereas for someone who is over 55 with an income of at least £40,000 a year the likelihood of voting is 79 per cent. In a study of government responsiveness to voter preferences in twelve West European democracies between 1973 and 2002, researchers concluded that

> parties display no tendency to respond positively to the vast majority of the public, namely the constituency of rank-and-file citizens who do not engage regularly in political discussion and persuasion. By contrast parties appear highly responsive to the viewpoints of opinion leaders, i.e., the relatively small subconstituency of citizens that habitually discuss politics and who attempt to persuade others on political issues.[1]

In a study of US senators' responsiveness to voters' policy preferences, it was found that 'senators are vastly more responsive to the views of affluent constituents than to constituents of modest means', and it is noted in passing that 'the fact that senators are themselves affluent, and in many cases extremely wealthy, hardly seems irrelevant to understanding the strong empirical connection between their voting

behavior and the preferences of their affluent constituents'.[2] Politics reproduces inequalities. Those
most in need of government help are the least likely
to contribute to the policy agenda, vote in elections
or be listened to by elected representatives. For the
most socially excluded and disadvantaged, the well-
rehearsed adage that 'whoever you vote for, the government always wins' still feels poignant.

These deficits point to a worrying gap between
the lofty principles of democracy and the practical
reality of everyday politics. Acknowledging this
does not amount to saying that democracy is a
sham and a fraud; that votes are not counted; that
governments are completely unaccountable to citizens; that there is no freedom of speech, assembly
and organization; or that elites can never be stopped
in their tracks by popular protest. It *is* to say,
however, that when democracy is experienced as a
political system in which most people feel removed
and distant from making decisions that will affect
their lives, political institutions are rarely trusted,
public debate is overwhelmingly shrill, partisan,
pugnacious and non-deliberative, and the actively
engaged are unrepresentative of the public at large,
there is something seriously awry.

A sense that political communication is failing to
serve democracy well is one of the few concerns that

unites both disengaged citizens and professional political elites. According to YouGov polling in April 2015, only one in four British voters in the lowest socio-economic group (DE) believed that democracy addressed their interests well, half as many compared to those in the highest socio-economic group (AB). Almost two-thirds of voters in the lowest socio-economic group said that democracy serves their interests badly, while fewer than one in ten believed that politicians understood the lives of people like themselves. In the same year a Pew Research Center poll found that 39 per cent of US voters agreed with the statement that 'voting by people like me doesn't really affect how government runs things' and nearly half (47 per cent) stated that 'there's not much ordinary citizens can do to influence the government'.

Meanwhile, political leaders and the pundits who scrutinize them acknowledge that the prospects for the kind of citizenship that would be worthy of democracy are shrinking. In his speech to the Illinois State General Assembly on 10 February 2016, President Obama observed that 'citizenship is threatened by a poisonous political climate that pushes people away from participating in our public life. It turns folks off. It discourages them, makes them cynical. And when that happens, more powerful and extreme voices fill the void.' Peter Oborne, a leading figure of the British radical right, has argued that members of the 'political class' have distanced themselves from ordinary people, express-ing themselves in a manner that is 'arcane, always self-referential, often concerned with the techniques of voter manipulation and relying on the anti-democratic assumption that there are matters which ordinary people are either incapable of understand-ing, or which it would be too dangerous for them to know'.[3] In his 2016 TED talk, former Greek Finance Minister Yanis Varoufakis suggested that citizens are right to regard politics as somewhat irrelevant, for 'we have confined...democracy to the political sphere, while leaving the one sphere where all the action is – the economic sphere – a completely democracy-free zone'.

These anxieties have provided a conspicuous back-drop to early twenty-first-century politics. Manifested most dramatically by the recent waves of populist anti-politics and theocratic anti-humanism that have sought to blot out the legacies of Enlightenment sen-sibility, but also by the atrophying of trust and deepen-ing of disenchantment that are slowly bleeding the civic lifeblood, the steady withdrawal of the *demos* from democracy has prompted much elite soul-searching. Contemporary governance is increasingly dependent not only upon the periodic consent of voters, but also upon active public participation in tackling a range of weighty problems that are beyond formal government authority, such as climate change, defence against terrorism and risks to public health. But such collaboration is thwarted by public suspicion that governments do not know how to listen to people; that co-governance is more about co-option than reciprocal communication. Conferences have been organized and reports published with a view to exploring the sources of this political malaise. Well-funded campaigns designed to 'connect with citizens' (especially the youngest ones) have been initiated. Some speak of a crisis of democratic legitimacy that makes it extremely difficult for governments to take bold actions in the name of people who have little faith in them. This malaise was succinctly captured by *The Economist* magazine, that bastion of orthodox opinion, when on 1 March 2014 it asked the question, 'What's Gone Wrong with Democracy?'

The great compromise

One answer to *The Economist*'s question is that the public is simply not up to the job of performing a central role within the drama of democracy. Except as voters who are invited every few years to 'support or oppose the individuals who actually govern',[4] the general public should not be expected to become embroiled in the political sphere. For, it is implied (and sometimes explicitly declared), they are too prone to reliance upon convenient prejudices; too susceptible to the vulgar charms of populist dema-gogues; too inclined to vote in TV talent shows rather than in elections for their local council; too fickle and disloyal for leaders to be able to rely on them; too coarse and brutal in their expression; and, of course, too unappreciative to recognize when they are being led by a more refined intelli-gence. Few political commentators these days overtly oppose the principle of democracy, but that does not stop them from responding with conde-scending irascibility when they encounter people talking about politics as if their voices mattered.

For example, when the right-wing journalist Rod Liddle refers to the Internet as 'a fugue of almost unrelieved idiocy, malice, spite, misinformation, banalities, lunacies, non-sequiturs and tedious vapidi-ties . . . rather than an Empowering Weapon for the Dispossessed Masses',[5] he is not really criticizing a particular technology. It is 'the masses' he finds distasteful; their loud voices, ill-formed opinions and not infrequent anger that irritate him online no less than they do offline. Like generations before him, Liddle's position seems to be that mass democracy is a fine ideal, if only the masses would shut up.

Indeed, it is only relatively recently that democracy has been embraced by political elites. There was an earlier consensus that nothing could be more intolerable than the prospect of democratic rule. Both of the towering figures of nineteenth-century British politics were self-declared anti-democrats. The Liberal leader William Gladstone asserted that 'if by democracy be meant the enthroning of ignorance against knowledge, the setting up of vice in opposition to virtue, the disregard of rank...then, ...I for one...am in that sense an enemy of democracy'.[6] The Conservative leader Benjamin Disraeli declared that 'I trust it will never be the fate of this country to live under a democracy.' If democracy were to be established, he warned,

> There will be no charm of tradition; no prescription spell; no families of historic lineage; none of the great estates round which men rally when liberty is assailed; no statesmanship, no eloquence, no learning, no genius. Instead of this you will have a horde of selfish obscure mediocrities, incapable of anything but mischief, and that mischief devised and regulated by the raging demagogue of the hour.[7]

By the mid-nineteenth-century, when the prospect of votes for all men seemed imminent, Thomas Carlyle noted that 'Everywhere immeasurable Democracy rose monstrous, loud, blatant, inarticulate as the voice of Chaos.' It was his opinion that 'it is the everlasting privilege of the foolish to be governed by the wise; to be guided in the right path by those who know it better than they'.[8]

Driving such rhetorical intemperance was a genuine fear of the 'masses' or the 'mob' – as they were irreverently labelled – who were considered lacking in either the cognitive or aesthetic potential to play anything but a subordinate part in the national culture. The newly enfranchised majority was described variously as 'a species of ape', the 'unintelligent classes' and 'a vast, featureless, almost shapeless jelly of human stuff...occasionally wobbling this way or that as some instinct of hate, revenge, or admiration bubbles up beneath it'.[9]

Despite these offensive reservations, universal franchise won the day – but it did so on the basis of a compromise. As Walter Bagehot, the most prominent theorist of the English Constitution, put it when writing about the political role of the newly enfranchised public: '[N]otwithstanding their numbers, they must always be subject, always at least be comparatively uninfluential. Whatever their capacity may be, it must be less than that of the higher classes, whose occupations are more instructive and whose education is more prolonged.'[10] Persisting into our own time, this compromise has conceived democracy as a politically bounded notion, relating to the election and accountability of responsible representatives, but not to the terms of cultural worth, which continue to depend upon undemocratic assumptions that some individuals possess habits, tastes and skills that are inherently superior and that the purpose of mainstream cultural institutions (the arts, higher education, public-service broadcasting and privatized schooling) is to foster the appreciation and perpetuation of these culturally foundational practices. Political democracy as we have come to experience it in most countries is characterized by a parsimonious code that values all voices equally for one brief plebiscitary moment every few years and the rest of the time accommodates itself to the structural economic inequalities and culturally self-replicating hierarchies that underpin a deeply undemocratic social order.

At the heart of this compromise is the continuing characterization of the non-elite as 'the masses': that amorphous mush of impersonal, unrefined mediocrity that stands as a permanent threat to culture. The masses are those people whose presence must be acknowledged, but not respected; who are the neighbours from hell so easily ridiculed on cheap TV documentaries and the target of advertisers wanting to sell shoddy merchandise. Raymond Williams astutely stated that 'There are in fact no masses, but only ways of seeing people as masses.' The masses are the *demos*, degraded through the lens of condescension. As Williams argued, 'I do not think of my relatives, friends, neighbours, colleagues, acquaintances, as masses; we none of us can or do. The masses are always the others, whom we don't know, and can't know.'[11] The prevailing compromise has at its core a belief in the radical separation of disparate qualities of lived experience and the consequent impossibility of the kind of reciprocal communication that could sustain democratic deliberation.

It fell to television, as the new predominant communication medium of the mid-twentieth century, to reconstitute the masses as audience. How did this happen? And to what extent can current hopes for the Internet be understood as a reaction to the 'audience democracy' that television ushered in?[12]

Television as a democratic good?

Television aroused great hopes that it could bring people together; reach those who were hitherto

43

excluded from literate culture; expose people to broad knowledge and pluralistic values; simplify complex issues; and foster tolerance. The earliest television sets were sold to the public with a breathless utopianism. A 1956 RCA cinema advertisement spoke of how

> One day, through television, the entire world will stream into our living rooms with the velocity of light. Not too far beyond the horizon, international television. To span oceans; capture all the visual beauty of far lands; bind people of all nations, tied together by better understanding, better knowledge, through instantaneous communication of sight and sound.[13]

Writing about the Apollo 11 moon landing, Milton Shulman rejoiced in the way that television coverage had brought the world together: 'It was shared at exactly the same moment by monarchs, dictators, heads of state and tycoons – no matter how rich or powerful – with the humble mechanic in Tokyo and the poorest Mexican grape-picker in California.'[14] The consequences for political democracy hardly required elaboration. 'It seems certain that television offers an unexampled source for...the political education of the nation as one community,' wrote one of the first American scholars to explore the new medium.[15]

But for critics of 'mass culture', television was little more than a 'children's medium' on which 'the young have become the acknowledged resident experts'. Unsettlingly, the new medium led to 'reduced time spent in conversation' and 'interaction among family members'.[16] Critics of the new medium pointed to its vulgarizing thrust. W.H. Auden declared that 'I don't see how any civilized person can watch TV, let alone own a set.' In an article entitled 'Can Democracy Survive Television?' one academic claimed that 'As the flow of complex political information declines apace with the increasing reliance on television as a source of political information, first the perceived need, and later the ability, to perform sophisticated intellectual operations on such information, as well as the complexity of politics itself, will also decline.'[17] Stated more directly by another commentator on the new medium,

The sad truth seems to be...that relatively few people in any society, not excluding Periclean Athens, have reasonably good taste or care deeply about ideas. Fewer still seem equipped – by temperament and capacity, rather than education – to handle ideas with both skill and pleasure. The deficiencies of mass media are a function, in part at least, of the deficiencies of the masses.[18]

Reading the debate about television and democracy, one is struck by the relentless dualism of the analysis and its uncanny similarity to current critiques of digital politics. It was as if a new communication technology had to be either a panacea for the failings of the social order or a malignant contributor towards cultural decay. One of the few balanced assessments in those early days came from Jay Blumler, who had little patience for intellectuals who accused the media 'of conditioning and debasing taste, of promoting shallow and hedonistic values, of fostering a cult of violence…and in general of propagating a synthetic culture'. Lamenting the failure of this debate to 'get anywhere', Blumler suggested that

> This failure may be linked with the self-centred tone of much of the discussion. That is, the cultural debate chiefly reflects the efforts of intellectuals to come to terms with media that seem to project standards differently from those that they have learned to respect. Consequently, the argument sheds more light on the anxieties and needs of intellectuals than on the place of the media in the lives of most of the public….[19]

Indeed, what often passed as a critique of television amounted to a grumbling disapproval of its audience. Like the masses before it, the audience was a discursive construction, an attempt to abstract embodied viewers from their complex social contexts and objectify them as a nebulous aggregation. The television audience stood as an object to be addressed, worked upon, measured, sold to advertisers, informed for its own good and culturally satiated. The television industry imagined this audience as a target to be reached, while critics of television imagined it as being unreachable by anything but the lowest common denominator. Neither of these perspectives acknowledged the possibility that audience members, as citizens, might possess their own democratic agency. Both conceived of televised politics as something to be transmitted for mass reception; a relentless monologue rather than a multi-vocal conversation. (In reality, of course, television audiences are much more actively involved in negotiating the meaning of texts, based upon the context of reception and their reasons for watching.[20])

Television started out as an observer of political events, reporting on the exercise of power and providing public accounts that could help to explain how the political game worked, but came over time to define the rules of the game. Politicians are now expected to adapt to its communicative logic, presenting themselves for scrutiny by interviewers and commentators who claim to be speaking for the public. Election campaigns have become battles for the attention of the cameras; policies are shaped by spin doctors charged with assessing how they will play on television; qualification to govern is confused with on-screen credibility. These moves in the direction of *audience democracy* have left citizens confused, struggling to distinguish between authentic values and media performances. This unease is exacerbated by systemic collusion between political and media elites who are locked into a self-referential discourse focused on winning the game, often regardless of any duty to provide credible evidence for their claims. There is a growing feeling that televised politics, far from opening up a democratic sounding board for public debate, has become little more than a tediously predictable spectacle, consigning its imagined audience to the role of silent extras whose experiences and values can be reduced to polling data.

Teledemocracy to the rescue?

Long before the Internet became available, news audiences began to vote with their remote controls, with some retreating altogether from the relentless flow of political messages, while others hoped to find new techniques and spaces through which politics could be recovered for democracy.

A number of pre-Internet experiments with what became known as *teledemocracy* attempted to explore the possibility of using communication technologies to develop participatory forms of political democracy. Some saw local cable television, with its capacity for broadband interactivity, as a way of returning agency to viewers:

> [M]embers of the audience would no longer be simply the passive recipients of mass communications messages but would participate actively in their selection and dissemination....Thus, direct feedback could well result in the reversal of the traditional roles of mass communications, making the communicator little more than a common carrier in a communications process controlled by each individual subscriber.[21]

Growing convergence between computers, telecommunications and interactive cable television prompted a number of initiatives intended to involve citizens directly in policy-making. In 1972 Amitai Etzioni developed the MINERVA (Multiple Input Network for Evaluating Reactions, Votes and Attitudes) project, designed to enable 'masses of citizens to have discussions with each other, and which will enable them to reach group decisions without leaving their homes or crowding into a giant hall'.[22] The system involved telephone conferencing, radio, two-way cable TV and satellites. In the 1980s a number of 'televote' experiments were conducted in Honolulu, Hawaii, and Southern California, in which random groups of citizens were contacted by telephone, invited to study a brochure containing policy information and varied opinions and then asked to vote on a policy question. Other projects utilized interactive technologies to provide direct channels of communication between citizens and government officials.

In a balanced analysis of these teledemocracy initiatives, F. Christopher Arterton identified five potentially democratizing characteristics of the new technologies: firstly, that they reduce the costs and increase the speed of information dissemination; secondly, that they vastly increase the number of available channels for the exchange of messages; thirdly, that such expansion could lead to a greater diversity of voices capable of addressing the public; fourthly, that they help communities bound by specialist interests to stay in touch with one another; and, fifthly, that they enable forms of interactive communication that transcend the categories of interpersonal and mass communication and might be referred to as 'semiprivate' or 'semipublic' communication.[23] Each of these features was subsequently to be ascribed to the Internet. What was at stake in these experiments, however, was more than a test of the deterministic affordances of technologies. More significantly, they were tests of what it means to be a political actor. For, as well as technological determinism (the belief that technologies can independently generate social effects), there is political determinism (the belief that relationships of power can only be organized or contested in one way). The teledemocracy experiments raised important questions about whether political agency could be enacted in different ways – questions that have become all the more relevant and urgent in the context of the digital media ecology.

Put simply, such experiments in political communication encourage us to consider what democracy could be like if citizens were imagined as neither amorphous masses nor consuming audiences. For any attempt to reinvigorate political contestation is bound to involve an imaginative effort to reconceive democratic agency in terms of heterogeneous autonomy.

Political Hopes and Fears

Beyond 'masses' and 'audiences'

To imagine citizens as something other than 'masses' is to make three claims about them. Firstly, it is to claim that they are capable of thinking about and acting upon the world as reflective individuals rather than an impulsive herd incapable of transcending socio-demographically determined pathways. As democratic agents, citizens are capable of mediating between their experience as individuals and their position as social beings. They are neither sovereign egos nor prisoners of social structure, but social actors capable of purposive action. Unlike the imagined masses, whose thought can only be read through their unruly actions, democratic citizens engage in reflection and goal-setting as activities in their own right. Making space for democratic agency entails acknowledging that people are capable of intelligent reflection and respecting the diverse modes in which that takes place and comes to be expressed.

Secondly, as social – and often sociable – beings, democratic citizens are capable of arriving at collective judgements. They are open to influence, not because they are gullible, but because they are cooperative hunters and gatherers of useful knowledge. As well as developing collective intelligence, democratic agents are capable of joint purpose. When objectives and rationales compete, the political emerges. There can be political disagreement without democratic agency, but only when such agency exists can we expect citizens to own their disagreements and feel capable of acting upon them efficaciously.

Thirdly, democratic agency is a foundation for the subjective belief that, as a member of a polity, one can influence its decisions and outcomes. Democratic agency is not an end condition, but a contingent basis for the possibility of making a social difference. Democratic citizenship in this sense can be understood as an ongoing process whereby what is presented as being natural and inevitable is tested and new configurations are explored. Where democratic agency is unleashed, it is no longer so obviously apparent who should make decisions and who should obey them, who is an expert and who should keep quiet, and what are reasonable assumptions and what are ignorant prejudices.

To think of democratic citizens as something more than members of an amorphous audience, trapped within a sender–receiver model of political communication in which they are destined to consume whatever symbolic pap is put before them, entails acknowledging that they are situated within social contexts in which there is more going on than just 'watching the telly' or 'reading the paper'. As people engage with mediated messages, the attention they bring, meanings they derive and salience they attach to them are shaped much more by their environment, dispositions, memories and goals than by a linear path between themselves and media centres. Consequently, television viewers and newspaper readers frequently derive meanings from messages which defy the intentions of their senders.

For people are rounded social beings who bring life experiences to their engagement with the media rather than mere consumers who respond *en masse*. People have varying ideas about what they need to be capable of doing in order to function as democratic citizens. These capabilities might range from being able to understand what politicians mean when they use terms like 'austerity' or 'freedom', to being able to check the veracity of factual claims, to feeling able to communicate with people making decisions that will affect them. Democratic agency entails the possibility of articulating these needs and then taking action to realize them.[24]

The extent to which the Internet can help to strengthen democracy depends, then, upon its relationship to democratic agency. Does it enable democratic citizens to do things and develop capabilities that were less likely to be achieved in a pre-digital media ecology? This is an empirical question, but one that is unlikely to be answered by looking for simple, linear media effects. Much of the existing research on the Internet and politics has sought to discover correlations between various forms of Internet use and various kinds of participatory political behaviour. As will become clear in the next chapter, while some encouraging correlations have been found, they rarely point to causal relationships. It is best to proceed by assuming that the Internet *per se* does not make things happen. More interesting than the search for deterministic outcomes are studies that have explored how the Internet has been incorporated into people's daily lives in ways that have expanded the range of democratic acts they feel capable of performing. These might include searching for information, sharing content, circulating narratives, mashing up data, storing material, adopting innovative approaches to self-presentation, challenging authoritative claims, entering cross-cutting networks and playing with identity. Democratic agency in this sense is a matter of expanding the range of possibilities for making a social difference and spanning cultural boundaries that had previously seemed inviolable.

3

Democratic Limbo

Contemporary politics has a transitional and indeterminate quality, hovering uneasily between the national and the global, the centralized and the networked, the managed and the populist, and the analogue and the digital. Political practices that were once taken for granted are beginning to seem unstable and emergent modes of political articulation are unsettling complacencies. During the course of the twentieth century the consolidation of political democracies generated routine approaches to producing, processing and communicating political messages. This political communication system resulted in predictable relations between political elites, journalistic mediators and citizens. Four interrelated factors have profoundly disrupted this system.

The first emanates from the seismic consequences of globalization. As the core activities of social existence – economic, cultural and political – have come to be integrated in real time on a planetary scale, earlier notions of place-based and spatially bounded power seem to lack meaning. Nation states persist, not least because of their intense symbolic appeal, but their capacity to exercise sovereign power is constrained by global forces beyond their control. Politics and power have become increasingly decoupled. The most pressing social challenges, from climate change, pandemics and the drugs trade to unregulated migration, terror threats and conflicts of moral fundamentalisms, are beyond the political scope of any single elected government. Governments are increasingly preoccupied with aspects of social life that they are incapable of governing. Huge powers are assumed by largely unelected and unaccountable transnational bodies. Nationally constituted political processes acquire a peripheral status, often characterized by a grandiosity of political rhetoric that cannot disguise their irrelevance. Faced with the tension between parochial politics and global power, democratically inclined thinkers have found themselves looking for spaces in which the increasingly interconnected people of the world can hold global power to account.

Secondly, the institutions through which political power has traditionally been mediated have fallen into disrepair. Political parties, which are supposed to represent the interests, preferences and values of citizens and translate them into achievable policies, are beginning to look like peculiar associations of the unrepresentatively committed. Government institutions, which derive their legitimacy from the electoral consent of the people in whose name they act, seem incapable of developing communicative relations with people that reflect the expectations of everyday sociality in the digital era. The mass media – whose role is to hold the powerful to account; to provide citizens with information that allows them to make considered choices about matters that affect them; and to maintain a space for pluralistic public dialogue – are struggling to work out effective ways of talking to audiences that are now capable of talking back to them. In most democratic countries, mainstream parties, government bureaucracies and the mass media are the least trusted institutions. All of them are trying desperately to reinvent themselves; to appear more open to public input and less manifestly locked into a legacy of thinking of 'the masses' as a seducible audience rather than potential partners. While it is certainly still the case that established political parties generate influential policies, governments wield national power and the mass media are the main sources of reporting government activity, all of these practices appear to be pervaded by a lack of political confidence. It sometimes feels as if centralized parties, government bureaucracies and the mainstream media are historical holding operations, enduring because nothing has yet emerged to displace them.

Thirdly, hitherto distinct boundaries between public and private have become increasingly unstable and bedevilled by ambiguities between first-person experiences and universal concerns. Issues once regarded as domestic and intimate, such as family dynamics, personal identities, sexual relationships and aesthetic values, have been taken up as matters of public contestation. At the same time, issues once thought to be best confined to an impersonal political language of instrumental rationality are now often discussed in terms of experiential sensibility. Authenticity emerges as a register of dextrous mediation between the disparate visibilities of the new publicness. Previously conceived in terms of linear transmission, the political communication system has become porous, and the democratic project, once limited to a clearly delineated 'public sphere', seeps into innumerable areas of social interaction that cannot be easily categorized as public or non-public, political or non-political.

Fourthly, the structure of the media ecology, through which messages and meanings travel, has changed. Thirty years ago this ecology appeared to be fixed and permanent, especially in relation to the mediation of politics, with television at the centre and the press providing an interpretive surround. Of course, even then there existed several channels of counter-cultural communication, but these were ecologically peripheral. With the emergence of the Internet as a publicly accessible network by hundreds of millions of people, it is no longer possible to speak of the media as centralized, quasi-industrial disseminators of public knowledge to a mass audience. The emergence of digital communication technologies has seriously disrupted journalistic practices, weakened gatekeeping privileges, expanded agenda-setting, circumvented contrived information scarcity and opened up a vast space for autonomous public interaction. This new media ecology has not displaced the old media system, but reconfigured it, leaving centres of communicative power vulnerable to a range of voices that had previously been easy to marginalize or ignore. The characteristics of this new media ecology relate closely to the other disruptions outlined above:

digital media transcend national borders, making them hard to regulate and inherently suited to global message flows; their protean porosity makes them risky for control-obsessed political institutions; and their mediation between personal and public spaces and experiences contributes to a reconceptualization of the social.

Faced with uncertainty, political institutions have tended to dig in, sometimes replicating routine processes online in the name of digital democracy, hoping that this will curb the contagion. All politicians now agree that they must govern with and through the Internet, but few are clear about how to do so. Plans for digital governance tend to be piecemeal and incoherent, fluctuating between celebrating the latest platform, tool or device that seems to embody technocratic efficiency and lamenting the borderless ungovernability of digital space. We shall turn in the final chapter to a consideration of what a democracy in tune with the digital era might look like. But first we must direct our attention to the uncertain present. To what extent has the Internet changed politics – and specifically the role of citizens – since the first website was established in 1990? What can people do now that they could not do before?

In any society that can meaningfully be referred to as democratic, citizens must be capable of performing six communicative tasks. The first is the circulation of experience. Common culture is the product of shared experience, ranging from great national and global moments and events to the everyday patterns and rhythms of social interaction. The terms and tones of the mediation of collective experience determine the scope for democratic action. Individual, unshared thoughts or sensations can easily dissipate into solipsistic angst. For democracy to be realized, there must be a degree of common social recognition; an understanding of the countless ways in which the life of the self is related to the lives of others.

Secondly, even though democratic politics can work perfectly well without citizens following every twist and turn, and democratic citizens can get by without having an encyclopaedic knowledge of current affairs, people need to be able to gather reliable information so that they can at least have some idea of the main challenges facing their society, the range of conflicting views about those issues and the choices before them as voters. In reality, most people take information-gathering further than that, with a view to responding to social problems that affect them, seeking support for their values and preferences and feeling competent to engage in discussion with others. For democracy to work well, pluralistic sources of information must exist so that people can make their own sense of the world.

Thirdly, democracy depends upon the existence of discursive habits and mechanisms. People need to know what it means to 'have an argument', 'consider the evidence', 'negotiate a compromise' or 'agree to disagree'. For democracy to be meaningful, there must exist a recognized language of public disagreement. Without opportunities to reflect together, the public is vulnerable to manipulation by those who claim to speak in its name.

Fourthly, people need to be capable of bringing about social improvements and eradicating social injustices; of taking collective action in response to situations and experiences that are amenable to human control. To do so, they need to reach and connect with one another. Because social coordination is a vital precondition for any democratic act, access to communicative resources is an indispensable civic right.

Fifthly, people need to feel confident that centres of authority, be they political, corporate or civil, are responsive to public demand. Policies, rules and norms should not be established behind people's backs. When decisions are made by elected representatives as if the represented have no thoughts of their own or abilities to articulate them, there is a failure not only of ethical respect, but also of communicative opportunities to make meaningful inputs to policy formation and decision-making.

Sixthly, people must be able to scrutinize and evaluate policies once they have been implemented. This applies especially to those who are most likely to be affected by them. The sustainability of democracy depends upon the existence of robust modes of public appraisal that monitor democratic outcomes with a view to defining the salience of issues and the restructuring of subsequent policy processes. This calls for technologies of accountability and transparency that are embedded within structures of authority as a safeguard against the potentially corruptive effects of institutional seclusion.

In this period of turbulent transition, how well are citizens able to meet these communicative challenges? Are there examples of the Internet making it easier – or more difficult – for citizens to exercise democratic agency?

The circulation of experience

Because no two lives are the same, people tell stories through which they present themselves and their experiences to others. Such storytelling is not a mere pastime, but the expression of an existential need for recognition. When people tell stories about what happens in their lives, they are performing their identities; attempting to affect the ways in which they are thought of by others; and learning to see themselves as others seem to see them. Such reflexivity is a defining feature of modernity; people want to manage their own self-presentation rather than have their identities carved out for them. Within what has been called an attention economy there is an incessant battle for eyes and ears, determining who will rise to cultural and political visibility.[1] In such circumstances, being conspicuous is a form of social power and attention becomes a valued currency. This is the case not only for political elites soliciting public acknowledgement and endorsement, but also for any human being laying claim to a personal identity.

In the era dominated by broadcasting, the framing of public stories fell to a small number of media organizations, often driven by commercial and ideological interests at odds with the norms of democracy. There can be no doubt that the emergence of social networking sites such as Facebook, YouTube and Twitter has reconfigured the storytelling environment. The numbers alone are staggering:

Facebook has 1.65 billion user accounts, with 500,000 new people joining each day at a rate of six per second; on YouTube there are 300 hours of video content uploaded per minute and 3.25 billion hours viewed per month; on Twitter there are 500,000 tweets sent out each day at a rate of 6,000 per second and there are 320 million active users. What are these hundreds of millions of people doing, and what might their online actions have to do with strengthening democracy?

At the micro level, there is evidence to suggest that users are able to manage social relationships within online networks in ways that make it easier for them to make social connections with others.[2] For example, studies from the United States suggest that, compared to the average American, Facebook users are half as likely to be socially isolated, are more trusting of others and are much more likely to be politically engaged.[3] People who are connected to large personal online networks are more likely to engage in both formal and informal political actions.[4] Even more important than the size of online networks is their heterogeneity: that is, the extent to which they expose users to diverse experiences and opinions. The more that people encounter social networks comprising people unlike themselves, the more likely they are to be receptive to new political perspectives.[5]

At a macro-social level, the proliferation of online narratives helps to counter official and corporate attempts to shape the public agenda. The pre-digital media landscape was dominated by the industrial production and distribution of news. Authoritative political narratives emanated from centralized sources and were legitimized epistemologically by journalistic claims to objectivity. The centrality of broadcasting and the press as sources of narrative authority remains, even though they are increasingly likely to be accessed via digital platforms. While there is scant evidence to support claims that we are living in a post-broadcast era, it is certainly the case that the circulation of public experience is now beyond the editorial control of traditional journalism. The concept of 'news' is in transition, and political elites often find it necessary to respond swiftly to digitally circulating stories and issues that emerge beyond the comfort zones of their own mediacentric bubbles. There are two principal ways in which online stories trigger broader political agendas. The first occurs when the mass media pick up concerns, stories and debates that are circulating online, perhaps in the blogosphere or on Facebook or Twitter. Such spill-over effects are most likely to transpire when themes are raised by coalitions of actors capable of framing the significance of their

issues in terms that can be understood and repli-
cated by mainstream journalists.[6] A second path to
agenda-setting is rather less conspicuous. When
people use search engines such as Google to find
political information, they are at the same time
generating important information about what sort
of issues and ideas are salient to them. When search
issues trend on Google, political actors and mass-
media journalists are likely to pay attention, not
only to the subjects that interest people, but also to
the ways in which they formulate their search questions. As a crude indicator of changing political
perceptions, the Internet offers an impressionistic
picture of an informal public sphere – or, more
precisely, a map of intersecting public spheres.[7]
Increasingly, governments are turning to these representations of publicness as means of monitoring
the reception of services and policies.[8]

Information-gathering

Civic information is a public good. Anyone can
access it without depleting its availability to others.
But having access to information is not in itself of
much value unless its recipients can make sense of
it. An illiterate person locked inside a library will

be faced with the challenge of deciphering what would at first look like a vast mass of illegible data. People do not simply search for data, but also seek meaning. One criticism of the super-abundant store of digitally accessible information is that it exposes people to more data than they can possibly filter, without providing tools of interpretation that can translate them into knowledge. The formidable challenge for democracy is to empower citizens to turn recondite data into useful knowledge.

Some parts of the mass media contribute to such meaning-making, but critical attention has rightly been focused on arrogant and irresponsible 'news' providers that specialize in misinformation, distortion and old-fashioned propaganda.[9] Given that these are the most widely accessed information sources and agenda-setters in most consolidated democracies, hopes have been expressed that the Internet might provide an alternative conduit for political information-gathering. The speed and breadth of online information allow people to select, evaluate and process unprecedented volumes of information, as well as hyperlinking between contrasting accounts and pluralistic explanations. When people access media networks such as Facebook and Twitter, they are more likely to enter into political discussion with others, regardless of the usual socio-demographic barriers to political engagement.

Because the Internet offers citizens 'contact with diverse perspectives, opportunities for deliberation and exposure to civic resources and recruitment',[10] it provides an independent pathway to political socialization and participatory behaviour, separate from pre-Internet routes to engaged citizenship. This is a very important finding, for it suggests that, unlike with other information-seeking practices, where people select sources that reinforce their existing views, people who search for political information online are likely to be exposed to cross-cutting political perspectives, sometimes leading them to reconsider their original positions.[11] One should not, of course, be too sanguine about this finding: it is based on aggregate accounts of information-seeking practices by the significant minority of people who connect to online social networks. For others, online sources are accessed selectively, much like pre-digital news media, thereby reinforcing group polarization.[12]

Democratic discussion

Politics exist because interests, preferences and values vary, often in ways that elude painless conciliation. From parliaments and town meetings to pub arguments and voluble gatherings around dinner tables, official and informal deliberative exchanges take place all the time. It is hardly surprising that, given the ubiquity of the Internet, many of those political discussions have now migrated online. Some commentators dismiss online political talk as vacuous garrulity. Others argue that there are features of online communication that could enhance the quality of public discussion and temper the incivility of headline-dominated discourse. For example, asynchronous discussion spaces in which there is time to reflect before responding, the availability of hypertextual links to background information and the presence of digital platforms designed to encourage reciprocal communication might afford opportunities for better-informed democratic discussion.

Two contrasting findings arise from studies of online political talk. Firstly, where spaces for online discussion of political issues are carefully designed and structured, often as experimental projects, participants tend to behave in ways that are more consistent with democratic norms than in offline discussion. Research has found that online deliberators are more open to considering and embracing a broadened repertoire of arguments and evidence;

more likely to change their minds about where they stand; and likely to retain their more reflective judgements months after the discussions conclude.[13] (However, the quality of online discourse deteriorates markedly in highly partisan contexts, which manifest identical characteristics to offline polarized spaces.[14])

The second finding is that it is rare for online political discussion to be meaningfully integrated into institutional processes of policy formation or decision-making. To put it bluntly, most online political talkers speak only to themselves. Even when online discussions provide insightful narrative perspectives, valuable (often local) evidence and coherent accounts of how discrete arguments relate to one another, political decision-makers fail to engage with them in more than tokenistic ways. While government institutions have committed considerable resources to the organization of online consultative exercises, it is uncommon for these to incorporate elements of structured public deliberation, or even informal peer-to-peer talk of a kind that is ubiquitous on social media. As a consequence, online deliberation, where it works well, tends not to have obvious political influence (leading some deliberating citizens to question its value), while online public interactions that are promoted by governments rarely encourage citizen-to-citizen dialogue, less still anything that democratic theorists would recognize as deliberation.

Apart from institutionally connected politics, there is compelling evidence to suggest that even when online discussion is more extemporaneous, informal and unsupported by any kind of deliberative infrastructure, participant behaviour is often much closer to deliberative norms than might be expected.[15] What is the point of such political talk? Firstly, it bridges the gap between what can easily be dismissed as mundane, politically irrelevant talk about music, football, soap narratives or private values, on the one hand, and views about the distribution and exercise of social power, on the other.[16] Such talk can lead people to recognize the presence of the political within what they might have first regarded as purely personal talk. Secondly, it enables people to address other citizens with a view to influencing public opinion. There is evidence to suggest that people are more likely to feel efficacious in relation to horizontal (peer-to-peer) effects than vertical (citizen-to-government) influence.[17] Thirdly, political talk, even when it is only for its own sake, has epistemic benefits, especially when, through porous online networks, people are exposed to views and experiences that they did not set out to encounter.

Collective action

As was discussed in the opening chapter, there is compelling evidence to suggest that the Internet has diminished many hitherto intractable barriers to the coordination of collective action. Opportunities to engage in what some scholars are calling 'connective action' have lowered the costs of protest as well as affecting the morphology of informal political expression. This has resulted in tangible gains for certain under-resourced communities and populations, and while entrenched structural inequalities continue to stratify opportunities to organize collectively, there is growing evidence to suggest that social media networks afford scope for the development of group identities and the conduct of informal activism.[18] However, celebratory accounts of online political networking have tended to focus upon the mobilization of democratic energy rather than its translation into policy outcomes.

Since the nineteenth century, the classical linking mechanism between public demands and governmental actions has been political parties. In the main, these institutions have been slow to respond to the digital media ecology, sometimes trying to shrug off the Internet as if it were an unruly pest, at other times venturing online to replicate long-established strategies of top-down message delivery. Parties have been in precipitous decline for some years, in terms of both membership and public affiliation. Nonetheless, they perform several crucial roles within representative democracy: aggregating interests and preferences and articulating them as a single package; reducing political complexity by simplifying the policy choices on offer; and providing an ongoing link between citizens and elected representatives. Loose and potentially ephemeral social movements cannot perform these linkage roles, firstly because their mobilizing strength is partly derived from the very absence of clearly defined, binding goals, and secondly because their appeal as informal associations makes it very difficult to establish or uphold durable democratic structures.[19] It may well be that political parties as we knew them in the twentieth century are now obsolete, but they are unlikely to be effectively replaced by loose mobilizing networks that cannot provide sustained mediation between public demands and representative responses.

Some advocates of Internet-enabled democracy have turned to the potential of the Wikipedia model as a way of conducting government. For example, one former adviser to the Obama administration has argued that 'collaborative democracy aspires to the kind of intentional peer production and shared group effort of Wikipedia, in which volunteers sign up to write encyclopedia entries as a group. While crowdsourcing activities like prediction markets aggregate individual preferences, collaboration implies more robust and diverse coordinating structures that enable people to divvy up roles.'[20] As a contribution to the division of labour within networked governance, what has been referred to as wiki government may be promising, but it remains unclear how political disagreements can be worked through in such a context. The collaborative editorship of Wikipedia is mainly focused upon policing the epistemological boundaries between justifiable and unfounded claims. Truth claims in relation to politics are much fuzzier and, because conflicting interests are involved, aspirations to arrive at a collectively validated consensus rather miss the point. The search for a mechanism that can combine the power of networked coordination with the articulation of competing interests has proved to be elusive and will continue to be so unless advocates of technocratic governance come to terms with the inevitability that political conflicts have no single, 'correct' conclusion, but can only ever be contested and resolved as battles of competing interests.

Consultation and public inputs

The effectiveness of democratic representatives depends upon there being an unambiguous relationship between the actions they take and the will of the represented. It is usually forgotten that Edmund Burke, when he argued in his famous 1774 'Speech to the Electors of Bristol' that representatives should not be mere delegates bound by constituent mandates, went on to say that 'it ought to be the happiness and glory of a representative to live in the strictest union, the closest correspondence, and the most unreserved communication with his constituents. Their wishes ought to have great weight with him; their opinion, high respect; their business, unremitted attention.' In short, even where democracy is based on electoral representation rather than direct plebiscites on all issues, the relationship between citizens and those elected to speak for them depends upon ongoing and respectful communication in both directions. Without it, representative claims could easily degenerate into strategic manipulation and the legitimacy of representative institutions would atrophy. (In many respects, this is precisely what has happened to contemporary political representation.)

The Internet has provided representative institutions with an opportunity to bolster their legitimacy by entering into a more ongoing communicative relationship with citizens. Rather than rely upon single electoral mandates, expressed once every few years, political representatives can invite the public to provide their own inputs into the policy process. It could be argued that this turn to a more consultative democracy is a pragmatic response to the decline of mass political parties; if the latter can no longer claim to aggregate and articulate public opinion, consulting directly with communities and individuals provides a new means of mediating the citizen–representative relationship. Governments and legislatures have engaged in a range of innovative practices designed to solicit public comment and experiential testimony online – although, as we saw in chapter 1, institutional timidity has often resulted in a preference for seeing citizens as enthusiastic observers rather than active interlocutors.

From the late 1990s onwards, initiatives aimed at gathering online policy inputs have been trialled. The UK Parliament's online consultations invited people to contribute their ideas and experiences on a range of issues, including domestic violence, hate crimes in Northern Ireland, flood protection, embryo research and the role of women in science.[21] But these initiatives have not been sustained or institutionalized; they have mainly served as digital add-ons to traditional structures which have no way of translating them into policy outputs. Less promisingly, governments have turned to e-petition technologies to allow people to sign up to collective requests and demands. In the most detailed evaluation to date of the UK government's e-petitions site, Scott Wright reflects that the

> Downing Street e-petitions did not achieve a high level of considered judgement. Most petitioners gave limited information to support their petition, and there was no formal space for debate or to counter-petition....While there were a small number of cases where e-petitions influenced policy, the vast majority disappeared into a vacuum and this was reflected in the perceptions of petition creators.[22]

Scrutiny

Even if the communicative challenges outlined so far are frustrated, one final opportunity remains available to democratic citizens: the right to hold power-wielders to account. Governments might fail to listen to people, arrive at ill-informed decisions and implement policies that seem unjust and unjustifiable, but they can rarely escape the wrath of an offended citizenry. According to the political theorist Pierre Rosanvallon, the most important political function of the Internet lies not in its capacity to facilitate participation and deliberation while policies are being made, but 'in its spontaneous adaptation to the functions of vigilance, denunciation and evaluation'. Indeed, the Internet 'is not merely an "instrument"; it *is* the surveillance function'.[23] At an institutional level, the Internet makes it much more difficult than it once was to operate in whispers, hide embarrassing information, cover up failed projects and deliver one message to one audience and a quite different one to others. The Internet changes the terms of visibility, if not democratizing it, as some have rather excitedly claimed, at least making the playing field more level. In terms of individual behaviour, the Internet makes it much harder to manage political images. Old distinctions between the political front- and back-stage are now unstable, as Labour Prime Minister Gordon Brown learned to his cost when he appeared to be having an amicable conversation with an elector a few days before the 2010 UK general election, only to discover that his 'private' irritation that he later expressed at her alleged bigotry was picked up by a microphone and relayed as evidence of his 'real' thoughts.

Internet transparency combines intentional moves to release selected data, once deemed to be secret or at least non-public, and involuntary disclosure, in which governments are caught out by the unintended public appearance of material they had wanted to remain publicly invisible, often as a result of active interventions by data hackers. This has produced a peculiar political tension, with liberally inclined governments celebrating their commitment to open data and insisting that there is both a cultural and economic value to allowing people to access and contribute to government data, while traditional preoccupations with secrecy and backstage flexibility lead those same governments to obsess about data protectionism. In the United Kingdom, the MySociety social enterprise is a great example of a small body of tech-savvy democrats who specialize in being online irritants, but constructive ones, forcing governments to acknowledge and act upon public acts of scrutiny. Having devised a range of innovatively designed tools – including WriteToThem, which allows people to make direct contact with their Member of Parliament and monitors their responsiveness; WhatDoTheyKnow, which processes freedom of information requests; and FixMyStreet, which enables people to report needed repairs to local authorities –, MySociety has worked hard to ensure that open data are put to democratic uses.

At the same time, the Internet has enabled entirely new forms of scrutiny, such as WikiLeaks, which leave governments feeling vulnerable at their most sensitive diplomatic core. A single memory stick containing almost 400,000 documents was released into the public domain. According to two British journalists who worked on the data to convey their meaning, WikiLeaks marked 'the end of secrecy in the old-fashioned, cold-war-era sense'.[24] The subsequent Snowden revelations added to this sense of government impotence in the face of digital scrutiny.

All of this leads back to the first communication challenge facing democratic citizens: letting others know who they are and why their experiences matter. Efforts to hold governments to account are a mirror reflection of the same impulse. All democracy is ultimately about making things visible; not only events and processes, but relations, attitudes and assumptions. Over the past two decades the

Internet has been implicated in the emergence of a new approach to social visibility. It has made it harder for authorities to depend upon communicative entitlements that once made them appear so implacable. And yet the transition to something different seems to be radically incomplete. It is as if we are stuck in a moment when democracy is neither sustainable as it stands nor moving in any manifestly progressive direction. Within this vacuum, toxic currents are simmering.

4

Populism or Democracy?

Political democracy is in serious trouble, lacking convincing moral authority in the face of post-truth politics and relentlessly threatened by populist fantasies. From Donald Trump's pledge to build a mighty wall to keep out foreigners to Brexit promises to eradicate the effects of globalization while remaining part of the global market; from religious fundamentalist invocations of medieval dogma as a retreat from the complexities of modernity to the toxic drip of scapegoating propaganda by the tabloid news media, populists pander to the latent delusions of the socially injured.

As an ideological perversion of democracy, populism is based upon the myth of the common-sense public taking on the corrupt elite. Who needs evidence or expertise when, for populists, the simple truth is obvious? Who needs debate when doubters are manifestly weird or venal? Who needs well-constructed arguments when chantable slogans are more memorable? Confusing mass malleability for informed consent, populist leaders act as if democratic agency were a disposable frill. Posing as an expression of general will, populism dissolves the public into an amorphous mass: dummies spoken for by demagogic ventriloquists.

While mainstream politicians are untrusted, populist leaders are over-trusted, for they embody public fantasies and echo the disappointment, rage and quick-fix logic of the audiences that cheer them on. Populism thrives upon a toxic mixture of frustrated democratic capacity and grandiose political ambition. Its demagogic heroes urge their followers to smother their impotence with their desires. The early twenty-first century has witnessed the global march of the populists, but also the subsequent chagrin of those who invested hope in them.

If a way out of this political morass is to be found, it will surely entail a fresh approach to understanding citizens as something more than pliable political consumers.

To speak of citizens as possessing democratic agency is not to suggest that they are straining at the leash to become intensely politically engaged.

Most people want a quiet life. They care mainly about political decisions that affect them. They do not want to spend hours each day pondering over economic statistics, think-tank reports and draft legislation. They understand that making good decisions is hard work and often involves trade-offs and even ethical compromise. A very small minority of people are politically knowledgeable and passionate. A similar minority are almost totally disengaged, not only from the political sphere, but sometimes from society in general. Most people – including the present writer – hover between working hard to manage their personal lives and being intelligently concerned about the society they inhabit, at both the global and neighbourhood levels. If it is not to dissipate into fruitless reverie, reimagining the way we mediate democracy will need to be tempered by a pragmatic balance between lofty idealism and mundane practicality. It must serve the needs of not only the politically engaged and technologically savvy, but also the vast majority of people who sense a basic discrepancy between their disappointing experience of flawed political democracy and their belief that something better is surely possible.

Often new political realities are heralded not by grand declarations, but by newly inflected ways of speaking about the world. Rather than thinking about the Internet as a constellation of clever technical devices or a mass of disparate content, we might think of it as a new space of public articulation; a multi-vocal arena in which no single standard of cultural status or evaluation of communicative literacy prevails. Despite sustained legal efforts to tame it and strenuous corporate endeavours to colonize it, the Internet remains a potential space of emergent self-expression.

Realizing that potential depends upon working out practical ways in which citizens can function as democratic actors. Faced with a global space within which one can lurk, troll, search, filter, connect or scream into the lonely void, the question arises, what do I need to be capable of doing and being if I am to function as a person who can exercise democratic agency? If the Internet is to play a part in strengthening democracy, this will depend upon the extent to which it expands the range of self-articulating moves that citizens feel able to make.

The previous chapter considered the extent to which the Internet has enabled citizens to behave in new or more effective ways within the current political communication system. But strengthening democracy is likely to require rather more than the application of digital add-ons to obsolete structures.

It entails rethinking the practice of democracy in the light of new communicative possibilities and rethinking ways and means of communicating in terms of hitherto unrealized democratic norms. The ideas set out in this chapter respond to this dialectical logic by focusing upon the ways in which democratic agency could be strengthened by acting *with and upon* technologies of digital mediation.

This entails thinking about democratic capabilities and, specifically, what citizens need to be able to do in order to be autonomous, informed, reflective, efficacious social actors. There is a surface plausibility to Winston Churchill's quip that 'The best argument against democracy is a five-minute conversation with the average voter', but at a deeper level raises profound questions about the kind of relationship that could possibly exist between rulers and electors when the latter are characterized with such casual disrespect. The four areas of democratic capability-building outlined below are not intended to provide a conclusive blueprint for a stronger democracy. On their own, they do not touch on the deeply entrenched socio-economic structures that perpetuate cultural advantages and constrain political efficacy. That would call for a much more expansive manifesto in which the democratization of public communication would be urged in parallel with other radical enlargements of social justice. Nor do they address the much broader range of civic capabilities that are needed by people in areas of the world that are far from being consolidated democracies. If the approach taken here is regarded as being in any way useful, others will undoubtedly augment and revise the list of four primary democratic capabilities that are set out. The point of the following proposals is to consider what kind of democratic capabilities people need if they are to be free to act confidently and efficaciously within the seriously flawed political democracies that now constitute the majority of countries in the world.

Capability 1: being able to make sense of the political world

Citizens must be capable of knowing and showing who they are, but they must also know where they are and what is going on around them. The cartography of the political sphere is opaque. The temptation to disengage from making sense of it all is powerful. Much was said and written about the quality of the campaign surrounding the UK referendum on its continued membership of the European Union. The consensus seems to be that it was a bad-tempered debate in which excessive and injudicious claims left many voters feeling bewildered. In an age of post-truth politics, campaigners were free to make assertions that lacked any empirical foundation, often protected by impartiality rules that lead public-service broadcasters to offer equal time and respect to both sides in any public argument, regardless of their rational foundations. Few British citizens complained that nobody provided them with information about how to vote, but most felt overwhelmed by mixed messages and epistemic uncertainties. When it is not only doubted whether any one account of reality has greater veracity than any other, but also believed that any procedure for arriving at truth is as good as any other, the scope for arriving at universally meaningful normative responses to social injustice is seriously imperilled. Without the potential for shared political purpose, democratic politics is reduced to a mechanism for managing cultural fragmentation and incomprehension.

In dealing with the sheer speed of unfolding social reality, citizens are poorly served by journalistic interpreters. The 24/7 news cycle, while enabling journalists to cover stories as they transpire, typically results in unreflective accounts of what events mean. Facile, misleading and psychologically unsettling, the non-stop torrent of news and information generates a political pace that is out of kilter with everyday life, and particularly with the uniquely human capacity for reflective thought. The mass media pander to a one-dimensional democracy in which the rich drama of voting provides a constant source of material, while opening up time and space for the slower, gentler, more contemplative process of debating evidence and forming judgements is too often treated with casual indifference.[1]

Concerns about the temporal challenges facing politics have been expressed by social theorists who fear that 'with the development of networked electronic information technologies that operate at near the speed of light the pre-conditions for temporal control have been eliminated'. It is claimed that instantaneous information transfer across global space has been achieved 'at the expense of hundreds of years of advancements in efforts to control the uncontrollable and predict the unpredictable'.[2] Most of the excellent literature on politics and speed has tended to focus on problems of governance, where desynchronization between political decision-making and cultural pace leads to a kind of organizational giddiness. It has been suggested, for instance, that the speed of digital communication in crisis situations may well enable governments to keep up with ground-level volatility, but might also push them into making rash, ill-judged decisions with negative long-term consequences.

Anxieties about loss of temporal control are by no means confined to elite decision-makers. Celebratory accounts of digital political activism tend to focus on the creative agility of the techno-savvy. Mainly young, middle-class and confident in the cultural fast lane, these are the people who not only tweet occasionally, but also follow Twitter trends; for whom web 2.0 is not just a technical step change but a communicative identity; who share files and manage feeds and dart casually between digital platforms. They are, however, a minority, not only of national populations, but also of Internet users within those populations. While this minority tend to feel quite relaxed about the stress of being permanently connected to others, the pressures of information overload and the risk of losing control in a technologically saturated environment, the majority of Internet users are rather less sanguine. For them, the digital world begins to feel rather like being in the constant presence of a fast-talking salesman who has something to say about everything, but has little that is meaningful to convey about anything.

The Internet offers unprecedentedly abundant information to those who have time to look for and digest it, but people commonly report feeling over-whelmed by data overload. They worry that with all these bits and bytes coming at them relentlessly, the world is moving too fast for them to make proper sense of what is happening. The problem of information overload refers to people's different capacities to devote attention to the range of media content that is available to them. This is not simply a quantitative problem of there being too much 'stuff' and too many contexts in which it can be found. It also describes a qualitative cultural change, pressurizing people to make frequent filtering choices about what really matters to them; to spend more time than they have available making uncer-tain assessments of the value and credibility of information; and to arrive at faster decisions, driven by the uncontrollable speed of data flows. These pressures trigger anxieties and they exacerbate polarization between the digitally confident few and everyone else.

Counter-intuitive as it may seem, a valuable con-tribution that the Internet could make to democracy would be to decelerate exposure, allowing people time to think about what trends and events mean; to work out what they think about them; and to hear from others who interpret information differ-ently. Few people would buy a house on the basis of hearing a fast-talking, uninterrupted pitch from a person with an interest in selling it. They would want time to look around, compare it with other houses and take advice from friends and experts. Think, then, of an election campaign and the ways in which voters are urged to select a government. The speed of the pitch runs counter to calm reflection: a semiotic bombardment rather than a reasoned appeal. Sometimes people go online to check on what they have been told during the hurly-burly of the fast-moving campaign. This impulse to check, compare, weigh up and dissect could be better served. By designing digital resources that effectively slow down the democratic process and allow the majority of people who are neither political aficionados nor technological wizards to engage reflectively with political information, democracy could be made more inclusively accessible and intelligibly navigable.

The idea of slowing down democracy responds to recent theoretical work relating to dual-process thinking. According to behavioural economists such as Daniel Kahneman, humans tend to employ two modes of thinking: fast thinking, which is intuitive and requires minimal effort, and slow thinking, which is reflective and more cognitively demanding.[3] The argument is not that fast thinking should be replaced by slow thinking, for in many situations relying on what we already know and pursuing simple heuristic paths to what we need to know provide a sufficient basis for effective judgement. For example, crossing a busy road or deciding which television channel to watch are unlikely to be enhanced by slow thinking; it makes sense to do what comes intuitively in such situations. In other circumstances, however, such as making a big purchase or comparing complex options, slow thinking has great advantages. Political judgements of the kind facing people presented with radically competing claims about reality would certainly benefit from slow thinking. Because democratic politics as it has come to be experienced moves too quickly, characterized by fast-talking politicians, data gluts, ambiguous claims, even from experts, and journalistic interpretation that cannot always be trusted, there is a strong case for having a metaphorical pause button that allows people time to ask the right questions and evaluate meaningful answers.

Consider two examples of how the Internet has opened up such spaces of democratic deceleration. TheyWorkForYou.com is a website that provides rich information about representatives' voting records, expenses and speeches in the UK Parliament and also the Scottish Parliament and Northern Irish

Assembly. The 200,000–300,000 people who access the site each month are able to annotate written parliamentary proceedings and create customized newsfeeds about the latest appearances of individual members, as well as receiving email alerts on any item mentioning certain keywords. They also have access to video recordings of debates in the House of Commons which can be searched using verbatim, time-stamped transcripts. This is a remarkably successful democratic tool, with one in five of its users not having participated in politics at all in the year prior to using it and not being members of any political group. Given that MySociety, the non-profit organization that runs TheyWorkForYou.com, has access to only a small fraction of the funding available to official parliamentary and governmental websites, one can only imagine how much more expansive and detailed such digital monitoring could become if supported by appropriate democratic commitment. The value of this tool is that it allows citizens to take time exploring the ways in which they are being represented. Rather than having to keep up with obscurely placed reports of parliamentary proceedings, they can ask the kind of specific questions that matter to them. This is not necessarily an alternative to following the fast-moving news, but a personalized supplement to it.

Populism or Democracy?

A second project relating to slowed-down politics was initiated by a team of researchers from the University of Leeds and the Open University who worked on developing a way of allowing voters to make sense in their own time of televised election debates.[4] In 2015 seven UK party leaders took part in a two-hour televised election debate on ITV. Within minutes of it ending, polling companies declared 'who won' on the basis of asking viewers for their snapshot responses. Even before then, Twitter analysts were making claims about how voters were responding in real time. Everything was geared to instantaneous reactions. The Leeds/Open University research team, by contrast, designed a platform that would allow voters to re-watch the debate (or watch it for the first time), viewing all or any selected sections critically by being able to find answers to a range of questions about the sources and accuracy of the claims that debaters were making; the various performative strategies that the debaters employed; the extent to which their arguments were internally consistent and related to what other debaters were saying; and the live responses of viewers to their claims and performances. The assumption upon which this project was founded is that real-time exposure to a televised debate is probably not the best way to arrive at a final judgement about it. Slowing down the political process allows citizens to reflect not only upon information offered to them, but also upon the capabilities they need to make sense of complex questions.

Capability 2: being open to argumentative exchange

The political sphere seems to be dominated by the over-opinionated, who will not consider changing their minds, and the under-opinionated, who feel incapable of making up their minds. The former do not make good democratic citizens because their values and preferences are too rigid. The latter are problematic because either they are over-dependent on leaders to tell them what to do or they abstain from participation. The purpose of deliberation is to allow both of these groups of people (as well as the large number of citizens who have views, but remain open to persuasion) to be exposed to cross-cutting public discussion with a view to possibly arriving at refined perspectives. Many deliberative experiments have been conducted to see whether and how exposure to informed, respectful, inclusive discussion leads to preference shifting. One of the most encouraging findings from these has been that people are more likely to be intellectually flexible when thrown together with diverse strangers than when discussing ideas with people like themselves. In short, deliberative quality benefits from social heterogeneity.

From its earliest days as a public network, the Internet was regarded as a potential space for public deliberation. For similar reasons to the ones outlined by Arterton in his evaluation of the pre-Internet teledemocracy experiments discussed in chapter 2 (p. 50), theorists and practitioners believed that opportunities for large social groups to converse about public issues in well-designed online settings could improve the quality of democratic discourse. As stated in the previous chapter, there is considerable evidence to suggest that when representative groups (often referred to as mini-publics) are encouraged to reflect on difficult political issues within ideal deliberative environments, they tend to generate outcomes that meet normative democratic requirements. However, experimental projects involving mini-publics are little more than a form of laboratory democracy. Could deliberation become a more systemic feature of our politics?

To do so, it might be necessary to abandon some of the more demanding normative requirements associated with democratic deliberation and explore more effective ways of incorporating deliberative characteristics within the chain of macro-social discourse. Quite recently, deliberative theorists and practitioners have turned their attention to the notion of the deliberative system or ecology, by which they mean the interconnected but uncoordinated ways in which various institutions, media and civic arenas facilitate reflective formal and informal political talk.[5] The common thread running through a deliberative system – which might comprise entities as diverse as broadcasters, the press, online spaces, universities, schools, neighbourhood forums and parliaments – is the existence of practices likely to orient people towards taking a deliberative stance in relation to public affairs. There are several merits to this way of thinking about democratic deliberation. Firstly, it acknowledges the complexity of the democratic process. Political decision-making rarely takes place in the kind of temporally bounded, high-minded conditions typical of mini-public deliberation. Some aspects of a discursive culture can be deeply deliberative (such as select committees in the UK Parliament), while others will be routinely unreflective (such as tabloid newspaper editorials). By evaluating deliberation at the systemic level, one can balance strengths and weaknesses and consider their related effects. Secondly, thinking about a deliberative system allows for non-binary evaluations. Some elements of the system might fail to meet many of the normative prerequisites of deliberation, but still contribute particular discursive resources and opportunities that could support democratic capability-building. (For example, a reality TV series, conceived by its producers as anything but political or serious, might generate an important online debate about casual racism or transgender experience or everyday tactics for resisting omnipotent power.[6]) Thirdly, the deliberative system approach acknowledges that politics always entails a division of labour and, while rejecting the undemocratic notion of the unreflective 'masses' who should be permanently excluded from deliberation, recognizes that deliberative commitments, skills and outcomes are bound to vary across political contexts.

Building a more deliberative democracy at the systemic level would involve a radical re-design of the existing political communication system. For elected representatives and governmental institutions it would entail embracing a culture of listening and learning that is currently under-developed. One researcher who has extensively studied government claims to be listening to people (or 'stakeholders', as bureaucrats like to call them) observes that 'there is a marked and concerning lack of listening by organizations – government, corporate, and some NGOs and non-profits – in contemporary societies'. Indeed, he refers to this as a 'crisis of listening'.[7] For the mass media, the transition to a culture of listening would not only involve a departure from their instinct to manage discursive access, cover events episodically, over-frame narratives and frequently harangue audiences, but it would also call for a more creative approach to audience interactivity than they have yet been able to develop. Neither of these changes is likely to be made voluntarily, but that does not mean that they are unlikely to happen. Both political and media institutions are finding it extremely difficult to sustain themselves in their current forms; they will either be swamped by populism or have to adopt more expansive and inclusive codes and practices of argumentative exchange. It would be hard to imagine the Internet not playing a central part in this process.

There are several models to learn from here: the ways in which participatory budgeting exercises have been conducted within online spaces; the impressive online debates that fed into the rewriting of the Icelandic constitution in response to that country's economic implosion; and the proposal to establish an online civic commons as a trusted space where the dispersed energies, self-articulations and aspirations of citizens can be rehearsed, in public, within a process of ongoing feedback to the various levels and centres of governance: local, national and transnational.[8]

A number of specific designs for online deliberative spaces have been produced, including Unchat and Open DCN, both real-time discussion tools for small-group deliberation. The former features 'speed bumps', designed to force users to encounter relevant information prior to participating in debate. Transcripts are provided to help latecomers to 'catch up' with previous discussion. The Deliberative Community Networks (OpenDCN) project allows participants to upload their own background information in a wide array of formats, using built-in templates to supply their own datasets or links to external datasets. In this way, they are able to offer their own interpretations of evidence, thereby transcending the rather artificial distinction between background information and deliberative practice. The important point here is that these innovations need not be stand-alone; it is not a question of online or offline deliberation, but of both happening simultaneously within a deliberative system, with specific spaces and media contributing according to their specific affordances.

Only time will tell whether the trigger for establishing any of these models will be a bold political commitment to enrich democratic discourse or a stunned response to the next populist travesty. But it is hard to imagine existing political democracies avoiding grievous disruption by populist tendencies unless they begin to think seriously about their current deliberative deficits.

Capability 3: being recognized as someone who counts

The social theorist Axel Honneth has rightly argued that 'the moral quality of social relations cannot be measured solely in terms of the fair or just distribution of material goods; rather, our notion of justice is also linked very closely to how, and as what, subjects mutually recognize each other'.[9] Could the Internet constitute a global space in which the dynamics of recognition and respect can be played out? In a democracy seeking to abandon crude certainties about the nature of the public, few objectives could be more important than developing spaces in which pluralistic self-representation can be translated into effectual political representation.

The democratic citizen is faced with difficult questions: Who am *I* and how do I want to be seen? Who are *we* and where do *I* fit in to this amorphously aggregated *us*? Contemporary citizens speak of feeling both taken for granted and forgotten. Pre-determined labels of economic class, cultural status, ideological loyalty and gender and ethnic identities have traditionally labelled and placed people: 'natural Labour voters'; 'religious conservatives'; 'Brits'; 'Scots'; 'Europeans'; 'woolly liberals'; 'youth'. These simplistic nomenclatures do not accord with people's sense of who they are, and this has prompted new practices of self-representation, ranging from the banality of selfies to moving examples of digital storytelling in which rarely heard voices contribute to public discourse.[10] Through these practices, crudely aggregated accounts of 'the public' are called into question and groups that have been typically defined through media-framing characterize them-selves in more nuanced ways. For example, YouTube images of urban policing counter simplistic narra-tives of dutiful law enforcers versus unruly hood-lums. Military blogs cast doubt upon uncritical notions of war as heroic patriotism. Online diasporic communities show how migrants often come to be seen as foreigners in both their homelands and host states.[11] As these accounts circulate, it becomes more difficult to see the world through blunt-edged catego-ries; encountering the complexity of real experience undermines dogmatic certainty.

Populism or Democracy?

Driven by new-found enthusiasm for the collection of 'big data', governments have taken a recent interest in monitoring these disparate public accounts. They trawl Twitter and other social network sites with a view to 'reading' public sentiment. They generate elaborate graphs showing how government services and policies are talked about online. In some situations they attempt to stimulate online memes that will reflect well on them. (Businesses have been engaged in the same activities for much longer.) Apart from the flawed epistemological claims sometimes made by big data theorists,[12] the main problem with this approach to understanding the public is that it is essentially surveillant; the capacity of the state to keep traces on people's online movements vastly outweighs its commitment to interacting with them as democratic citizens. For all of the sophisticated sociograms produced by governments to identify who is saying what about which issue, hardly any serious efforts have been made to connect self-representation to the institutional work of speaking for, to and with the represented.

One might expect political parties to perform the role of expressing the socio-cultural diversity of the represented, but, by perpetuating homogeneous fictions regarding the unity of their supporters, they merely exacerbate the problem. As organizations built around centralized power, they regard their members' self-representation as high-risk deviations from disciplinary order. That is why the online presence of mainstream parties is generally considered to be at odds with the communicative openness of the Internet. There is an inherent mismatch between the voluble self-expression of people online and the attenuated character of partisan representation. Faced with a choice between reinvention and atrophy, most political parties are drifting towards the latter.

Historically, the organization of political rule has entailed a stark choice between direct democracy (everyone votes on every issue) and representative democracy (leaders are elected every few years to speak for people). In contemporary consolidated democracies there has been a constitutional accommodation to the latter. But the terms of this accommodation have not been refined for decades. The capacity that now exists for live interaction between represented constituencies and political centres makes it difficult to justify the detached relationships that prevail within contemporary political democracies. There is an understandable suspicion on the part of citizens that such distance reflects a failure of recognition and respect rather than an intractable problem of communication. When entire social groups, such as youth, the disabled and the poorest communities, are rendered politically invisible or only visible in one-dimensional ways, they are entitled to conclude that the promises of democratic representation do not apply to them.

Supported by well-designed digital communication structures and strong political will, representation could be reconceived as an ongoing conversation about local experiences, competing values and public choices.[13] Opportunities to send emails, texts and tweets to elected representatives, government departments and other centres of political authority already exist, with variable degrees of meaningful feedback provided. Beyond the simple act of posting a request or message, however, there is surely scope for a much richer form of political co-presence through which the public can 'achieve such recognition of itself as will give it weight'.[14]

There is no single design for making direct representation work, but some promising models exist, ranging from the informal decision-making networks that have evolved around the World Social Forum and Occupy movement to the grass-roots online democracy forums that were initiated two decades ago in Minnesota, and have since spread to other countries.[15] These networked formations raise important questions about the extent to which nineteenth-century constitutional structures characterized by executive command centres, parliamentary or congressional partisanship and a communicative gulf between representatives and the represented are compatible with emergent modes of decentralized governance.

As ambiguities have intensified in recent years between the boundaries of 'the social' and 'the political', interactive governance has emerged as a source of legitimate democratic representation.[16] By allowing citizens and communities to engage directly in the formulation of policy inputs and then gearing policy outputs towards the satisfaction of such felt needs, interactive governance confers a new kind of democratic legitimacy upon political authority. However, if interactive governance is primarily conceived in technocratic terms (for example, by limiting citizen inputs to the collection of polling data), it is likely to be regarded as tokenistic and potentially populist. For democracy to benefit from interactive governance, spaces of political articulation and consensus-building are needed that are trusted by both citizens and elected representatives. The Internet is a promising candidate as such a space, for it is broadly accessible – indeed, more so than ever before with the ubiquity of smartphones.

Direct representation online could combine the raw creativity of self-representative practices with a new constitutional architecture designed to capture public ideas and experiences at the right moments in the constitutional process.

The transition to interactive governance, both off- and online, faces formidable cultural challenges from institutional actors unable to reconcile bureaucratic order with dialogical communication. Enlarging and deepening the political sphere calls for some humility from citizens in the face of policy complexities and multi-level processes. Opening up governance to a much broader range of voices calls for similar humility from politicians and bureaucrats as they learn to share democratic space with increasingly knowledgeable, confident and demanding citizens. The development of mutual recognition and respect is not a mere precursor to democratic politics, but the very essence of politics, which entails an ongoing struggle to be counted as one who matters.

Capability 4: being able to make a difference

Democratic agency is a means rather than an end. That is to say, even if people were to develop capacities to represent themselves and be well represented; make meaningful sense of the world; and exchange opinions and ideas in a constructively deliberative fashion, they would still be faced with the political task of making a difference to the organization of social power and the allocation of values. For populists, making a difference is unequivocal and easily measured. Seeing themselves as the guardians of instinctive common sense, they aim to liberate politics from the necessity for disagreement and wrangling. Making a meaningfully democratic difference is a much more complex exercise because it entails a pragmatic acknowledgement that what is right and what is true are intrinsically contestable. Populists adopt what the philosopher Richard Rorty calls a 'final vocabulary': they know what things mean, and anyone who disagrees with them is implicated in a betrayal of moral certitude.

For democratic citizens, a principal challenge is to maintain a pluralistic presence, resisting homogeneous representations and insisting on the right to define (and redefine) themselves. Not only sweeping terms such as 'the people', 'the masses', 'the audience' or 'Internet users', but more specific tags, such as 'the angry white working class', 'do-gooding liberals', 'true believers', 'ethnic minorities' and 'fellow Americans', should be regarded with the greatest possible caution. It becomes clear after around thirty minutes of exploring how communities and individuals represent themselves online that human experience is nuanced, ambiguous and inconsistent. To be sure, experiential patterns are discernible, and these are commonly shaped by deep structural forces, but people do not apprehend their lives as one-dimensional outcomes of socio-economic structures.

Simply making the vibrant plurality of social presence visible is politically important, for two reasons. Firstly, because we are living through a period in which decisions are increasingly justified by nullifying ordinary voices. Perhaps the most potent belief of ascendant neoliberal ideology is that economic rationality can only prevail if billions of voices do not. In circumstances where almost every section of society apart from the very rich and institutionally powerful complains that its views are rarely taken into account, the simple act of maintaining a voluble presence is of great democratic value. Secondly, it is important that people resist allowing themselves to be defined and framed by mediators whose intentions are often far from democratic. The images of social reality perpetuated by the most widely read newspapers and the least

responsible broadcasters are mean, divisive and distorted. People are regularly depicted in unjust ways
on the basis of their class, skin colour, gender, sexuality, age and belief. Correcting such pernicious
accounts is a vitally important democratic act.
Despite corporate efforts to colonize it, the Internet
offers a space in which counter-narratives can
succeed and records be put straight. As public areas
of the physical landscape are increasingly enclosed,
services once geared to universal provision privatized and customs of free intercourse undermined,
opportunities abound for people to make their
digital presence felt.

Increasingly, this presence assumes a 'post-
demographic' form, with individual profiles and
social relations rendered observable through algorithmic traces.[17] For example, while individual users
of social network sites, such as Facebook or Insta-
gram, might attempt to construct a profile of who
they are and what they like, socio-demographic
analysis makes it possible to construct profiles on
the basis of usage data and network link patterns
that individuals and groups might not even have
been aware of themselves. The surveillant risks
associated with such algorithmic citizenship are certainly worrying, but at the same time they support
new kinds of political visibilities through which

dispersed groups – often comprising people hitherto unaware that they constitute a social group – can nurture solidarities. For example, markets (which are themselves symbolic abstractions) have long operated as omnipotent expressions of transnational power, leaving their subjects fractured and unconfident. Post-demographic profiling can reveal traces of common misrecognition and exploitation by markets amongst their hitherto disconnected victims, such as subjects of sweated labour, environmental hazards or unlawful mis-selling by banks and insurance companies. Once revealed, such shared digital profiles can enable collective subjectivities to be articulated.

The decentralized, informal, often ephemeral nature of digital political presence stands in stark contrast to traditionally centralized, rule-governed, permanent political parties. The future of democratic politics may well depend upon how the tension between these two forms is resolved. As argued in chapter 1, the problem with much digital activism is its apparent incapacity to sustain itself around a cluster of coherent policies consistent with expressible and shareable principles. Consequently, digital mobilization, while capable of making a difference here and there, lacks the durability required to govern on the basis of a stable programme. On the other hand, existing mainstream parties, which have become increasingly similar to one another in their managerial commitment to neoliberal dogmas, lack the capacity to mobilize enthusiastic support or maintain public trust. Faced with complex and urgent social problems linked to growing inequality, terrorism, climate change, pandemics, mass migration, unstable regimes and post-industrial decline, bland managerial politicians seem locked into Groundhog Day, endlessly repeating strategies that fail to make a discernible difference to most people's lives.

While representative democracy is likely to persist into the foreseeable future, instruments and strategies for enacting political change might not. Across consolidated democracies, old and new, outmoded ways of making a political difference are in decline and disarray. New ways of articulating and exercising democratic agency, often with support from digital tools and networks, are becoming pervasive. But the historical trajectory of these developments is far from clear.

Much depends upon how the *demos* is persuaded to see itself. If, as populist leaders and parties would have it, citizens are prepared to be spoken for – 'I am your voice', declared Donald Trump as he accepted the Republican nomination in July 2016 –,

115

then 'the new politics' will amount to little more than a modified iteration of the long-standing compromise between constitutional equality and socio-economic hierarchy. In such circumstances, the Internet will undoubtedly perform a pivotal role as an echo chamber in which the crowd noise of mesmeric consensus can be ventilated. Far from nurturing democratic capabilities, such a media environment would signal their absence, offering instead a vast outlet for frustrated yearnings.

There are many millions of people, however, who see populism as the ultimate betrayal of democracy and are actively seeking inventive resources that will enable them to be acknowledged as intelligent beings. They respond with some scepticism to claims by mainstream and populist politicians to speak for them, for they have become tired of being spoken for. They are deeply sceptical of the anodyne language of technocratic managerialism that has come to pervade contemporary politics. They feel diminished and disparaged by the division of communicative labour which categorizes socially unrepresentative elites as speakers and everyone else as the spoken for – or spoken about. Those who think in this way certainly do not form a conscious movement; nor do they share the same political views. More importantly, however, they are united by a sense – perhaps no more than just a shared feeling – that democratic values matter, not just as abstract principles, but as enablers of capacities they think they ought to possess. Could the Internet open up space for such citizens to flex their democratic muscles and take on both the established political elites who have taken them for granted for so long and the new brand of snake-oil salesmen who are filling the void created by compromised democracy?

In recent times this question has become far from abstract or academic. The ascendancy of populist leaders and programmes has unnerved many people who had until now assumed that democratic politics could withstand the illiberal allure of demagogy.

For a long time it was complacently assumed that the unheard would simply fade into sullen silence, interrupted by occasional bouts of vulgar pique and localized self-harm. Leave them alone; exclude them from the polling models because they won't vote; humour their audacious resentments and tell them what's best for them, from how to speak correctly to when to tighten their belts. Perhaps pay rhetorical lip service to the value of listening to them, while failing to acknowledge the unbridgeable chasm between tokenistic attention and sensitive comprehension.

Populism or Democracy?

We find ourselves living through an insurgency of the unheard. People who had not cast a ballot for years have voted for outcomes that the political pundits failed to predict. People whose votes were regarded as 'safe' have turned against parties and leaders who took them for granted. Political insiders who claimed to be experts at 'playing the game' have been shocked to discover that the rules have changed. New ways of talking about politics are emerging in defiance of the incestuous codes of technocratic management.

When British voters for Brexit yearn to 'take back control', they are expressing much more than a constitutional resentment about Brussels rule. They feel out of control. They have lost confidence in their capacity to perform as citizens capable of determining their own social future. When voters for Trump see themselves as 'the forgotten men and women of our country', the desire to be remembered – to count as someone worthy of being heard – runs deep. These cries for recognition reflect a longing for a new way of exercising political voice.

As has been stated repeatedly throughout this book, it would be naïve to assume that simply moving political communication online will either enrich or degrade the voices of democratic citizens. The old debate between Internet-Good and

Internet-Bad is pointless and redundant. But if popular democratic pressure for the kind of civic capacity-building outlined in this chapter were to gain traction, digital technologies, spaces and codes could play a significant role in facilitating practices conducive to a more inclusive, respectful and deliberative democracy.

Further Reading

This is certainly not the first book to consider the relationship between the Internet and democracy. Let me get my own books out of the way first: written with John Gotze, *Bowling Together: Online Public Engagement in Policy Deliberation* (Hansard Society, 2001) is a widely cited manifesto for democratic change. In *Direct Representation: Towards a Conversational Democracy* (Institute for Public Policy Research, 2005), I floated ideas that are developed in chapter 4 of this book. Written with Jay G. Blumler, *The Internet and Democratic Citizenship: Theory, Practice and Policy* (Cambridge University Press, 2009) set out a proposal for establishing a trusted online space for public deliberation. Two co-edited volumes are relevant to this book: with Peter M. Shane, *Connecting Democracy: Online Consultation and the Flow of Political Communication* (MIT Press, 2011); and with Deen Freelon, *Handbook of Digital Politics* (Edward Elgar, 2015). Finally, my book *How Voters Feel* (Cambridge University Press, 2013) provides a

Further Reading

theoretical foundation for much of what I have written in this book about the pressing need to rethink democratic practices.

There are many other fine books on this theme. The most brilliantly insightful, I think, is John Keane's *Democracy and Media Decadence* (Cambridge University Press, 2013), but the following are also worth reading: Manuel Castells' *Networks of Outrage and Hope: Social Movements in the Internet Age* (Wiley, 2015); Andrew Chadwick's *The Hybrid Media System: Politics and Power* (Oxford University Press, 2013); James Curran, Natalie Fenton and Des Freedman's *Misunderstanding the Internet* (Routledge, 2016); Peter Dahlgren's *The Political Web: Media, Participation and Alternative Democracy* (Palgrave Macmillan, 2013); Michael Jensen and Laia Jorba's *Digital Media and Political Engagement Worldwide: A Comparative Study* (Cambridge University Press, 2012); Douglas Kellner's *Media Spectacle and the Crisis of Democracy: Terrorism, War, and Election Battles* (Routledge, 2015); Robin Mansell's *Imagining the Internet: Communication, Innovation, and Governance* (Oxford University Press, 2012); Michael Margolis and Gerson Moreno-Riaño's *The Prospect of Internet Democracy* (Ashgate, 2013); Karen Mossberger, Caroline J. Karen, Caroline J. Tolbert and Ramona S. McNeal's *Digital Citizenship: The Internet, Society, and Participation* (MIT Press, 2007); W. Russell Neuman's *The Digital Difference: Media Technology and the Theory of Communication Effects* (Harvard University Press, 2016); Zizi Papacharissi's *A Private Sphere: Democracy in a Digital Age* (Polity, 2010) and *A*

Further Reading

Networked Self: Identity, Community, and Culture on Social Network Sites (Routledge, 2010); Matt Ratto and Megan Boler's *DIY Citizenship: Critical Making and Social Media* (MIT Press, 2014); and Christian Vaccari's *Digital Politics in Western Democracies: A Comparative Study* (Johns Hopkins University Press, 2013). Evgeny Morozov's *The Net Delusion: The Dark Side of Internet Freedom* (Public Affairs, 2012) will appeal to readers who like one-sided polemics.

The best book on the history of the Internet is Patrice Flichy's *The Internet Imaginaire* (MIT Press, 2007).

For further reading on problems of democratic representation (especially at the parliamentary level) and coordination considered in chapter 1, see Xiudian Dai and Philip Norton's *The Internet and European Parliamentary Democracy: A Comparative Study of the Ethics of Political Communication in the Digital Age* (Routledge, 2013) and Stephen Coleman, John Taylor and Wim van de Donk's co-edited *Parliament in the Age of the Internet* (Oxford University Press, 1999) on the former. On the latter, W. Lance Bennett and Alexandra Segerberg's *The Logic of Connective Action: Digital Media and the Personalization of Contentious Politics* (Cambridge University Press, 2013) is a magisterial work, but would be well supplemented by reading Bruce Bimber, Andrew Flanagin and Cynthia Stohl's *Collective Action in Organizations: Interaction and Engagement in an Era of Technological Change* (Cambridge University Press, 2012); Donatella Della Porta and Mario Diani's co-edited *The Oxford Handbook of Social Movements* (Oxford University Press, 2015); Helen Margetts, Peter

Further Reading

John, Scott Hale and Taha Yasseri's *Political Turbulence: How Social Media Shape Collective Action* (Princeton University Press, 2015); and, for a rather ideologically heavily laden study, Daniel Trottier and Christian Fuchs' *Social Media, Politics and the State: Protests, Revolutions, Riots, Crime and Policing in the Age of Facebook, Twitter and YouTube* (Routledge, 2014). Valuable as all these studies are, see Ulises Mejias's *Off the Network* (University of Minnesota Press, 2013) for a corrective to network-centrism.

For more about anti-democracy and the great democratic compromise discussed in chapter 2, see John Keane's *The Media and Democracy* (Polity, 1998) and *The Life and Death of Democracy* (Simon and Schuster, 2009). Jacques Rancière's *Disagreement: Politics and Philosophy* (University of Minnesota Press; 2004) is relevant, as are Ricardo Blaug's *Democracy, Real and Ideal: Discourse Ethics and Radical Politics* (SUNY Press, 1999) and Ronald Dworkin's *Is Democracy Possible Here? Principles for a New Political Debate* (Princeton University Press, 2006). On the much-contested relationship between television and democracy, the seminal study is Jay G. Blumler and Michael Gurevitch's *The Crisis of Public Communication* (Routledge, 1995). See also Brian Groombridge's *Television and the People: A Programme for Democratic Participation* (Penguin, 1972); Kurt and Gladys Lang's *Politics and Television* (Quadrangle Books, 1968); and Thomas Patterson and Robert McClure's *The Unseeing Eye: The Myth of Television Power in National Politics* (New York: Putnam; 1976). F. Christopher Arterton's *Teledemocracy: Can*

Further Reading

Technology Protect Democracy? (Sage Publications, 1987) is the key study on pre-Internet electronic democracy; see also Benjamin Barber's *Strong Democracy: Participatory Politics for a New Age* (University of California Press, 2003) and Theodore Becker and Crista Daryl Slaton's *The Future of Teledemocracy* (Greenwood Publishing Group, 2000). On audiences, see Ien Ang's *Desperately Seeking the Audience* (Routledge, 2006); Jean Burgess and Joshua Green's *YouTube: Online Video and Participatory Culture* (Wiley, 2013); Richard Butsch and Sonia Livingstone's *Meanings of Audiences: Comparative Discourses* (Routledge, 2013); and Michael Strangelove's *Watching YouTube: Extraordinary Videos by Ordinary People* (University of Toronto Press, 2010).

For further reading about the ways in which online citizens have been engaging with current political structures, discussed in chapter 3, consult the excellent scholarly journals that publish regular research updates on this subject. Amongst the best of these are *Information, Communication & Society*, *Information*, the *Journal of Computer-Mediated Communication*, the *Journal of Information Technology & Politics* and *New Media & Society*.

Chapter 4 focuses on democratic capabilities. For further reading on capabilities' theory, see David Crocker's *Ethics of Global Development: Agency, Capability, and Deliberative Democracy* (Cambridge University Press, 2008); Nicholas Garnham's 'Amartya Sen's Capabilities Approach to the Evaluation of Welfare: Its Application to Communications', in Andrew Calabrese and Jean-Claude Burgelman's edited collection *Communication,*

Citizenship, and Social Policy: Rethinking the Limits of the Welfare State (Rowman & Littlefield, 1999), pp. 113–24; Martha Nussbaum's *Creating Capabilities* (Harvard University Press, 2011); and Martha Nussbaum and Armatya Sen's *The Quality of Life* (Oxford University Press, 1993).

My own thinking about the four democratic capabilities outlined in chapter 4 is influenced by a broad range of intellectual sources. These include: Henrik Bang's *Governance as Social and Political Communication* (Manchester University Press, 2003); Nick Couldry's *Why Voice Matters: Culture and Politics after Neoliberalism* (Sage Publications, 2010); John Dryzek's *Deliberative Democracy and Beyond: Liberals, Critics, Contestations* (Oxford University Press, 2000); Axel Honneth's *Disrespect* (Polity, 2007); Daniel Kahneman's *Thinking, Fast and Slow* (Allen Lane, 2011); and John Parkinson and Jane Mansbridge's *Deliberative Systems: Deliberative Democracy at the Large Scale* (Cambridge University Press, 2012).

Notes

Chapter 1 The Great Missed Opportunity

1 Available online at http://www.digitaldemocracy.par-liament.uk/documents/Open-Up-Digital-Democracy-Report.pdf.
2 Ibid., p. 14.
3 Ibid., p. 73.
4 See, for example, Ted Becker and Christa Daryl Slaton, *The Future of Teledemocracy* (Greenwood Publishing Group, 2000); Dick Morris, *Vote.com* (Macmillan, 2011).
5 *Open Up!*, p. 28 (see note [1]).
6 Ibid., p. 49.
7 Ibid., p. 45.
8 Ibid., p. 49.
9 Ibid., p. 17.
10 Ibid., p. 33.
11 Ibid., p. 20.
12 Ibid., p. 18.

13 W. Lance Bennett and Alexandra Segerberg, *The Logic of Connective Action: Digital Media and the Personalization of Contentious Politics* (Cambridge University Press, 2013), p. 35.
14 Ibid., p. 24.
15 Jennifer Earl, Jayson Hunt and R. Kelly Garrett, 'Social Movements and the ICT Revolution', in Hein-Anton van der Heijden (ed.), *Handbook of Political Citizenship and Social Movements* (Edward Elgar, 2014), p. 368.
16 Manuel Castells, *Networks of Outrage and Hope: Social Movements in the Internet Age*, 2nd edition (Polity, 2015), p. 236.
17 Ibid.
18 Ibid.
19 See John Perry Barlow, 'A Declaration of the Independence of Cyberspace' (8 February 1996). Available online at https://w2.eff.org/Censorship/Internet_censorship_bills/barlow_0296.declaration.
20 John Keane, *Democracy and Media Decadence* (Cambridge University Press, 2013), p. 21.

Chapter 2 Political Hopes and Fears

1 James Adams and Lawrence Ezrow, 'Who do European Parties Represent? How Western European Parties Represent the Policy Preferences of Opinion Leaders', *The Journal of Politics* 71.1 (2009), p. 218.
2 Larry M. Bartels, 'Homer Gets a Tax Cut: Inequality and Public Policy in the American Mind', *Perspectives on Politics* 3.1 (2005), pp. 29 and 30.

3 *The Spectator*, 12 September 2007.
4 Walter Lippmann, *The Phantom Public* (Transaction Publishers, 1927), p. 62.
5 *The Spectator*, 4 January 2014.
6 *The Times*, 7 April 1866.
7 *Hansard Parliamentary Debates*, 27 April 1866.
8 *Latter-Day Pamphlets 1: The Present Time* (1 February 1850), p. 13.
9 William Inge, Virginia Woolf and W.B. Yeats, respectively, quoted in John Carey, *The Intellectuals and the Masses: Pride and Prejudice among the Literary Intelligentsia 1880–1939* (Faber & Faber, 1992), pp. 25 (Inge and Woolf) and 14 (Yeats).
10 Walter Bagehot, *Parliamentary Reform: An Essay*, Vol. 20 (Forgotten Books, 2013 [originally 1857]), p. 18.
11 Raymond Williams, *Culture and Society* (Chatto & Windus, 1959), pp. 11 and 29.
12 Bernard Manin, *The Principles of Representative Government* (Cambridge University Press, 1997).
13 Accessed at https://www.youtube.com/watch?v=qhqt ByYjmPY.
14 *Evening Standard*, 14 July 1971.
15 Charles Alexander Holmes Thomson, *Television and Presidential Politics: The Experience in 1952 and the Problems Ahead* (Brookings Institution, 1956), p. 168.
16 George Comstock, 'The Impact of Television on American Institutions', *Journal of Communication* 28.2 (1978), p. 23.
17 Jarol B. Manheim, 'Can Democracy Survive Television?' *Journal of Communication* 26.2 (1976), p. 87.

18 Leon Rosten in Norman Jacobs, *Culture for the Millions? Mass Media in Modern Society* (Van Nostrand, 1961), p. 72.

19 Jay G. Blumler, 'British Television – The Outlines of a Research Strategy', *The British Journal of Sociology* 15.3 (1964), pp. 223–4.

20 See Ien Ang, *Desperately Seeking the Audience* (Routledge, 2006); Jay G. Blumler and Elihu Katz, *The Uses of Mass Communications: Current Perspectives on Gratifications Research* (Sage Publications, 1974); Robert Kubey and Mihaly Csikszentmihalyi, *Television and the Quality of Life: How Viewing Shapes Everyday Experience* (Routledge, 2013); Helen Wood 'Active Audience and Uses and Gratifications', in Manuel Alvarado, Milly Buonanno, Herman Gray and Toby Miller (eds), *The Sage Handbook of Television Studies* (Sage, 2014), pp. 366–84.

21 Don R. Le Duc, *Cable Television and the FCC: A Crisis in Media Control* (Temple University Press, 1974), p. 5.

22 Amitai Etzioni, 'MINERVA: An Electronic Town Hall', *Policy Sciences* 3.4 (1972), pp. 457–74.

23 F. Christopher Arterton, *Teledemocracy: Can Technology Protect Democracy?* (Sage Publications, 1987), pp. 29–38.

24 For a more detailed account of democratic capabilities, see Stephen Coleman and Giles Moss, 'Rethinking Election Debates: What Citizens Are Entitled to Expect', *The International Journal of Press/Politics* 21.1 (2016), pp. 3–24; Nicholas Garnham, 'Amartya Sen's Capabilities Approach to the Evaluation of

Welfare: Its Application to Communications', in Andrew Calabrese and Jean-Claude Burgelman (eds), *Communication, Citizenship and Social Policy: Rethinking the Limits of the Welfare State* (Sage, 1999), pp. 113–24.

Chapter 3 Democratic Limbo

1 Richard A. Lanham, *The Economics of Attention: Style and Substance in the Age of Information* (University of Chicago Press, 2006).
2 Nicole B. Ellison, 'Social Network Sites: Definition, History, and Scholarship', *Journal of Computer-Mediated Communication* 13.1 (2007), pp. 210–30; Nicole B. Ellison, Charles Steinfield and Cliff Lampe, 'Connection Strategies: Social Capital Implications of Facebook-Enabled Communication Practices', *New Media & Society* 13.6 (2011), pp. 873–92.
3 Joanna Brenner, 'Pew Internet: Social Networking' (2012), Pew Internet and American Life Project. Available online at http://www.pewinternet.org/2012/10/19/social-media-and-political-engagement/.
4 Homero Gil de Zúñiga, Aaron Veenstra, Emily Vraga and Dravan Shah, 'Digital Democracy: Reimagining Pathways to Political Participation', *Journal of Information Technology & Politics* 7.1 (2010), pp. 36–51.
5 Gary Tang and Francis L.F. Lee, 'Facebook Use and Political Participation: The Impact of Exposure to Shared Political Information, Connections with Public Political Actors, and Network Structural

Heterogeneity', *Social Science Computer Review* 31.6 (2013), pp. 763–73.

6 Barbara Pfetsch, Silke Adam and Lance W. Bennett, 'The Critical Linkage between Online and Offline Media: An Approach to Researching the Conditions of Issue Spill-Over', *Javnost – The Public* 20.3 (2013), pp. 9–22.

7 Gerard Goggin, Fiona Martin and Timothy Dwyer, 'Locative News: Mobile Media, Place Informatics, and Digital News', *Journalism Studies* 16.1, pp. 41–59; ByungGu Lee, Jinha Kim and Dietram A. Scheufele, 'Agenda Setting in the Internet Age: The Reciprocity Between Online Searches and Issue Salience', *International Journal of Public Opinion Research* 28.3 (2016), pp. 440–55; Jonathan Mellon, 'Internet Search Data and Issue Salience: The Properties of Google Trends as a Measure of Issue Salience', *Journal of Elections, Public Opinion & Parties* 24.1 (2014), pp. 45–72; Richard Rogers, 'Mapping Public Web Space with the Issuecrawler', in Bernard Reber and Claire Brossaud (eds), *Digital Cognitive Technologies: Epistemology and the Knowledge Economy* (Wiley, 2010), pp. 89–99.

8 Andrea L. Kavanaugh, Edward A. Fox, Steven D. Sheetz, Seungwon Yang, Lin Tzy Li, Donald J. Shoemaker, Apostol Natsev and Lexing Xie, 'Social Media Use by Government: From the Routine to the Critical', *Government Information Quarterly* 29.4 (2012), pp. 480–91; Rob Kitchin, 'The Real-Time City? Big Data and Smart Urbanism', *GeoJournal* 79.1 (2014), pp. 1–4; Panagiotis Panagiotopoulos, Alinaghi Ziaee

Bigdeli and Steven Sams, 'Citizen–Government Collaboration on Social Media: The Case of Twitter in the 2011 Riots in England', *Government Information Quarterly* 31.3 (2014), pp. 349–57; Mehmet Zahid Sobaci and Naci Karkin, 'The Use of Twitter by Mayors in Turkey: Tweets for Better Public Services?', *Government Information Quarterly* 30.4 (2013), pp. 417–25.

9 Steven Barnett and Judith Townend, '"And What Good Came of It at Last?" Press–Politician Relations Post-Leveson', *The Political Quarterly* 85.2 (2014), pp. 159–69; Matt Carlson and Dan Berkowitz, '"The Emperor Lost His Clothes": Rupert Murdoch, *News of the World* and Journalistic Boundary Work in the UK and USA', *Journalism* 15.4 (2014), pp, 389–406; Nick Davies, *Flat Earth News* (Random House, 2011); Daya Kishan Thussu, 'The "Murdochization" of News? The Case of Star TV in India', *Media, Culture & Society* 29.4 (2007), pp. 593–611.

10 Dhavan V. Shah, Jaeho Cho, William P. Eveland and Nojin Kwak, 'Information and Expression in a Digital Age: Modeling Internet Effects on Civic Participation', *Communication Research* 32.5 (2005), p. 537.

11 Jennifer Brundidge, 'Encountering "Difference" in the Contemporary Public Sphere: The Contribution of the Internet to the Heterogeneity of Political Discussion Networks', *Journal of Communication* 60.4, pp. 680–700; Jihyang Choi and Jae Kook Lee, 'Investigating the Effects of News Sharing and Political Interest on Social Media Network Heterogeneity',

Computers in Human Behavior 44 (2015), pp. 258–66; Yonghwan Kim, 'The Contribution of Social Network Sites to Exposure to Political Difference: The Relationships among SNSs, Online Political Messaging, and Exposure to Cross-Cutting Perspectives', *Computers in Human Behavior* 27.2 (2011), pp. 971–7; Yonghwan Kim, Hsuan-Ting Chen and Homero Gil de Zúñiga, 'Stumbling upon News on the Internet: Effects of Incidental News Exposure and Relative Entertainment Use on Political Engagement', *Computers in Human Behavior* 29.6 (2013), pp. 2607–14; Emily K. Vraga, Kjerstin Thorson, Neta Kligler-Vilenchik and Emily Gee, 'How Individual Sensitivities to Disagreement Shape Youth Political Expression on Facebook', *Computers in Human Behavior* 45 (2015), pp. 281–9.

12 Shanto Iyengar and Sean J. Westwood, 'Fear and Loathing across Party Lines: New Evidence on Group Polarization', *American Journal of Political Science* 59.3 (2015), pp. 690–707; Thomas J. Leeper, 'The Informational Basis for Mass Polarization', *Public Opinion Quarterly* 78.1 (2014), pp. 27–46; Cass R. Sunstein, 'Neither Hayek nor Habermas', *Public Choice* 124:1–2 (2008), pp. 87–95; Cass R. Sunstein, *Republic.com 2.0* (Princeton University Press, 2009).

13 Young Min Baek, Magdalena Wojcieszak and Michael X. Delli Carpini, 'Online versus Face-to-Face Deliberation: Who? Why? What? With What Effects?', *New Media & Society* 14.3 (2012), pp. 363–83; Todd Davies, 'The Blossoming Field of Online Deliberation', in Todd Davies and Seeta Peña

Ganghadran (eds), *Online Deliberation: Design, Research, and Practice* (University of Chicago Press, 2009), pp. 1–19; Dennis Friess and Christiane Eilders, 'A Systematic Review of Online Deliberation Research', *Policy & Internet* 7.3 (2015), pp. 319–39; Shanto Iyengar, Robert C. Luskin and James S. Fishkin, 'Facilitating Informed Public Opinion: Evidence from Face-to-Face and Online Deliberative Polls'. Available online at https://pcl.stanford.edu/common/docs/research/iyengar/2003/facilitating.pdf; Peter Muhlberger and Lori M. Weber, 'Lessons from the Virtual Agora Project: The Effects of Agency, Identity, Information, and Deliberation on Political Knowledge', *Journal of Public Deliberation* 2.1 (2006), pp. 1–37; Vincent Price and Joseph N. Cappella, 'Online Deliberation and Its Influence: The Electronic Dialogue Project in Campaign 2000', *IT & Society* 1.1 (2002), pp. 303–29.

14 Kevin A. Hill and John E. Hughes, *Cyberpolitics: Citizen Activism in the Age of the Internet* (Rowman & Littlefield Publishers, Inc., 1999); Matthew W. Hughey and Jessie Daniels, 'Racist Comments at Online News Sites: A Methodological Dilemma for Discourse Analysis', *Media, Culture & Society* 35.3 (2013), pp. 332–47; Marcin Lewiński, 'Collective Argumentative Criticism in Informal Online Discussion Forums', *Argumentation and Advocacy* 47.2 (2010), pp. 86–106; Ian Rowe, 'Civility 2.0: A Comparative Analysis of Incivility in Online Political Discussion', *Information, Communication & Society* 18.2 (2015), pp. 121–38; Anthony G. Wilhelm,

Democracy in the Digital Age: Challenges to Political Life in Cyberspace (Psychology Press, 2000).

15 Todd Steven Graham, 'What's *Wife Swap* Got to Do with It? Talking Politics in the Net-Based Public Sphere' (Ph.D. thesis, Amsterdam School of Communication Research, 2009); Edith Manosevitch, Nili Steinfeld and Azi Lev-On, 'Promoting Online Deliberation Quality: Cognitive Cues Matter', *Information, Communication & Society* 17.10 (2014), pp. 1177–95; Jakob Svensson, 'Participation as a Pastime: Political Discussion in a Queer Community Online', *Javnost – The Public* 22.3 (2015), pp. 283–97; Scott Wright, Todd Graham and Daniel Jackson, 'Third Space, Social Media and Everyday Political Talk', in Axel Bruns, Gunn Enli, Eli Skogerbø, Anders Olof Larsson and Christian Christensen (eds), *The Routledge Companion to Social Media and Politics* (Routledge, 2016), pp. 74–88.

16 Todd Graham, Daniel Jackson and Scott Wright, 'From Everyday Conversation to Political Action: Talking Austerity in Online "Third Spaces"', *European Journal of Communication* 30.6 (2015), pp. 648–65; Scott Wright, 'From "Third Place" to "Third Space": Everyday Political Talk in Non-Political Online Spaces', *Javnost – The Public* 19.3 (2012), pp. 5–20.

17 Stephen Coleman, David E. Morrison and Simeon Yates, 'The Mediation of Political Disconnection', in Kees Brants and Katrin Voltmer (eds), *Political Communication in Postmodern Democracy* (Palgrave Macmillan, 2011), pp. 215–30.

18 Shelley Boulianne, 'Social Media Use and Participation: A Meta-Analysis of Current Research', *Information, Communication & Society* 18.5 (2015), pp. 524–38; Sebastián Valenzuela, 'Unpacking the Use of Social Media for Protest Behavior: The Roles of Information, Opinion Expression, and Activism', *American Behavioral Scientist* 57.7 (2013), pp. 920–42; Anne Marie Warren, Ainin Sulaiman and Noor Ismawati Jaafar, 'Understanding Civic Engagement Behaviour on Facebook from a Social Capital Theory Perspective', *Behaviour & Information Technology* 34.2 (2015), pp. 163–75.

19 Anastasia Kavada, 'Creating the Collective: Social Media, the Occupy Movement and Its Constitution as a Collective Actor', *Information, Communication & Society* 18.8 (2015), pp. 872–86; Anastasia Kavada, 'Email Lists and Participatory Democracy in the European Social Forum', *Media, Culture & Society* 32.3 (2010), pp. 355–72.

20 Beth Simone Noveck, *Wiki Government: How Technology Can Make Government Better, Democracy Stronger, and Citizens More Powerful* (Brookings Institution Press, 2009), p. 18.

21 Stephen Coleman, 'Connecting Parliament to the Public via the Internet: Two Case Studies of Online Consultations', *Information, Communication & Society* 7.1 (2004), pp. 1–22; Stephen Coleman, 'The Internet as a Space for Policy Deliberation', in Frank Fischer and Herbert Gottweis (eds), *The Argumentative Turn Revisited: Public Policy as Communicative Practice* (Duke University Press, 2012), pp. 149–79.

22 Scott Wright, 'Assessing (e-)Democratic Innovations: "Democratic Goods" and Downing Street
e-Petitions', *Journal of Information Technology &
Politics* 9.4 (2012), p. 466.

23 Pierre Rosanvallon, *Counter-Democracy: Politics in
an Age of Distrust*, trans. Arthur Goldhammer (Cambridge University Press, 2008), p. 70.

24 David Leigh and Luke Harding, *WikiLeaks: Inside
Julian Assange's War on Secrecy* (Public Affairs,
2011), p. 183.

Chapter 4 Populism or Democracy?

1 Stephen Coleman, 'Debate on Television: The Spectacle of Deliberation', *Television & New Media* 14.1
(2013), pp. 20–30; Peter Dahlgren, *Media and Political Engagement* (Cambridge University Press, 2009);
Rousiley C.M. Maia, *Deliberation, the Media and
Political Talk* (Hampton Press, 2012).

2 Barbara Adam, *Time and Social Theory* (Wiley,
2013), p. 125. See also Robert Hassan, *Empires of
Speed: Time and the Acceleration of Politics and
Society* (Brill, 2009); Michael Saward, 'Agency,
Design and "Slow Democracy"', *Time & Society*,
online first: 4 May (2015); Andreas Schedler and
Javier Santiso, 'Democracy and Time: An Invitation',
International Political Science Review 19.1 (1998),
pp. 5–18; William E. Scheuerman, 'Busyness and
Citizenship', *Social Research* 72.2 (2005), pp. 447–
70; John Tomlinson, *The Culture of Speed: The
Coming of Immediacy* (Sage, 2007).

3 Daniel Kahneman, *Thinking, Fast and Slow* (Allen Lane, 2011). See also Keith E. Stanovich and Richard F. West, 'Individual Differences in Reasoning: Implications for the Rationality Debate', *Behavioral and Brain Sciences* 23 (2000), pp. 645–65; Gerry Stoker, Colin Hay and Matthew Barr, 'Fast Thinking: Implications for Democratic Politics', *European Journal of Political Research* 55.1 (2016), pp. 3–21.

4 Declaration of interest: I led this research team, which comprised Dr Giles Moss and Dr Paul Wilson (Leeds) and Dr Anna DeLiddo and Dr Brian Pluss (Open University). For more information about this project, see http://edv-project.net/. See also Michael Dale, Abram Stern, Mark Deckert and Warren Sack, 'Metavid.org: A Social Website and Open Archive of Congressional Video', in *Proceedings of the 10th Annual International Festival of Digital Government Research* (Digital Government Society of North America, 2009), pp. 309–10; Mark Deckert, Abram Stern and Warren Sack, 'Peer to PCAST: What Does Open Video Have to Do with Open Government?', *Information Polity* 16.3 (2011), pp. 225–41.

5 John Parkinson and Jane Mansbridge, *Deliberative Systems: Deliberative Democracy at the Large Scale* (Cambridge University Press, 2012).

6 Stephen Coleman, 'A Tale of Two Houses: The House of Commons, the Big Brother House and the People at Home', *Parliamentary Affairs* 56.4 (2003), pp. 733–58; Stephen Coleman, 'Acting Powerfully: Performances of Power in Big Brother', *International Journal of Cultural Studies* 13.2 (2010), pp. 127–46.

7 Jim Macnamara, *Organizational Listening: The Missing Essential in Public Communication* (Peter Lang, 2016), p. 314.

8 Jay G. Blumler and Stephen Coleman, *The Internet and Democratic Citizenship: Theory, Practice and Policy* (Cambridge University Press, 2009), chapter 8; Stephen Coleman and Rafael Cardoso Sampaio, 'Sustaining a Democratic Innovation: A Study of Three e-Participatory Budgets in Belo Horizonte', *Information, Communication & Society*, online first: 4 July (2016); Hélène Landemore, 'Inclusive Constitution-Making: The Icelandic Experiment', *Journal of Political Philosophy* 23.2 (2015), pp. 166–91; Tiago Peixoto, 'Beyond Theory: e-Participatory Budgeting and Its Promises for eParticipation', *European Journal of ePractice* 7.5 (2009), pp. 1–9; Bjarki Valtysson, 'Democracy in Disguise: The Use of Social Media in Reviewing the Icelandic Constitution', *Media, Culture & Society* 36.1 (2014), pp. 52–68.

9 Axel Honneth, *Disrespect: The Normative Foundations of Critical Theory* (Wiley, 2014), p. 130; see also Nick Couldry, *Why Voice Matters: Culture and Politics after Neoliberalism* (Sage, 2010).

10 Darcy Alexandra, 'Digital Storytelling as Transformative Practice: Critical Analysis and Creative Expression in the Representation of Migration in Ireland', *Journal of Media Practice* 9.2 (2008), pp. 101–12; John A. Bargh, Katelyn Y. McKenna and Grainne Fitzsimons, 'Can You See the Real Me? Activation and Expression of the "True Self" on the Internet', *Journal of Social Issues* 58.1 (2002), pp. 33–48;

Aline C. Gubrium, Eizabeth L. Krause and Kasey Jernigan, 'Strategic Authenticity and Voice: New Ways of Seeing and Being Seen as Young Mothers through Digital Storytelling', *Sexuality Research and Social Policy* 11.4 (2014), pp. 337–47; Carol Haigh and Pip Hardy, 'Tell Me a Story – A Conceptual Exploration of Storytelling in Healthcare Education', *Nurse Education Today* 31.4 (2011), pp. 408–11; Kerry M. Mallan, 'Look at Me! Look at Me! Self-Representation and Self-Exposure through Online Networks', *Digital Culture and Education* 1.1 (2009), pp. 51–6; Laura Robinson, 'The Cyberself: The Selfing Project Goes Online. Symbolic Interaction in the Digital Age', *New Media & Society* 9.1 (2007), pp. 93–110; Nitin Sawhney, 'Voices beyond Walls: The Role of Digital Storytelling for Empowering Marginalized Youth in Refugee Camps', in *Proceedings of the 8th International Conference on Interaction Design and Children 2009*, pp. 302–5; Jo A. Tacchi, *Finding a Voice: Digital Storytelling as Participatory Development in Southeast Asia* (Wiley-Blackwell, 2009); Nancy Thumim, *Self-Representation and Digital Culture* (Palgrave Macmillan, 2012); Sonja Vivienne, 'Trans Digital Storytelling: Everyday Activism, Mutable Identity and the Problem of Visibility', *Gay and Lesbian Issues and Psychology Review* 7.1 (2011), pp. 43–54.

11 Anat Ben-David, 'The Palestinian Diaspora on the Web: Between De-territorialization and Re-territorialization', *Social Science Information* 51.4 (2012), pp. 459–74; David Drissel, 'Digitizing Dharma:

Computer-Mediated Mobilizations of Tibetan Buddhist Youth', *International Journal of Diversity in Organisations, Communities & Nations* 8.5 (2008), pp. 79–92; Andrew John Goldsmith, 'Policing's New Visibility', *British Journal of Criminology* 50.5 (2010), pp. 914–34; Saskia Kok and Richard Rogers, 'Rethinking Migration in the Digital Age: Transglocalization and the Somali Diaspora', *Global Networks*, 1 April (2016); Bryce Clayton Newell, 'Crossing Lenses: Policing's New Visibility and the Role of Smartphone Journalism as a Form of Freedom-Preserving Reciprocal Surveillance', *Journal of Law, Technology and Policy* 1 (2014), pp. 59–104; Katy Parry and Nancy Thumim, '(Extra)ordinary Portraits: Self-Representation, Public Culture and the Contemporary British Soldier', *Media, War & Conflict* 9.1 (2016), 93–109; Brian P. Schaefer and Kevin F. Steinmetz, 'Watching the Watchers and McLuhan's Tetrad: The Limits of Cop-Watching in the Internet Age', *Surveillance & Society* 12.4 (2014), pp. 502–15.

12 Helen Kennedy and Giles Moss, 'Known or Knowing Publics? Social Media Data Mining and the Question of Public Agency', *Big Data & Society* 2.2 (2015), pp. 1–11; Ulises Ali Mejias, *Off the Network* (University of Minnesota Press, 2013).

13 Stephen Coleman, *Direct Representation: Towards a Conversational Democracy* (Institute for Public Policy Research, 2005).

14 John Dewey, *The Public and Its Problems: An Essay in Political Inquiry* (Pennsylvania State University Press, 2012 [originally 1927]), p. 77.

15 http://forums.e-democracy.org/about/localforums/; Sheetal D. Agarwal, Michael L. Barthel, Caterina Rost, Alan Borning, W. Lance Bennett and Courtney N. Johnson, 'Grassroots Organizing in the Digital Age: Considering Values and Technology in Tea Party and Occupy Wall Street', *Information, Communication & Society* 17.3 (2014), pp. 326–41; Jeffrey S. Juris, 'Reflections on #Occupy Everywhere: Social Media, Public Space, and Emerging Logics of Aggregation', *American Ethnologist* 39.2 (2012), pp. 259–79; Anastasia Kavada, 'Creating the Collective: Social Media, the Occupy Movement and Its Constitution as a Collective Actor', *Information, Communication & Society* 18.8 (2015), pp. 872–86; Anastasia Kavada, 'Engagement, Bonding, and Identity across Multiple Platforms: Avaaz on Facebook, YouTube, and MySpace', *MedieKultur: Journal of Media and Communication Research* 28.52 (2012), pp. 28–48.
16 Jaan Kooiman, Maarten Bavinck, Ratana Chuenpagdee, Robin Mahon and Roger Pullin, 'Interactive Governance and Governability: An Introduction', *Journal of Transdisciplinary Environmental Studies* 7.1 (2008), pp. 1–11; Milton L. Mueller, *Networks and States: The Global Politics of Internet Governance* (MIT Press, 2010); Jacob Torfing, B. Guy Peters, Jon Pierre and Eva Sørensen, *Interactive Governance: Advancing the Paradigm* (Oxford University Press, 2012).
17 Richard Rogers, *Digital Methods* (MIT Press, 2013), pp. 153–6. See also Heather Ford, 'Fact Factories: Wikipedia and the Power to Represent' (Doctoral dissertation, University of Oxford, 2015).